WINTER CROCHET
collection seven

CONTENTS

WINTER CROCHET

...is a celebration of the unique craft of crochet. Using Rowan Felted Tweed and Felted Tweed Aran, this timeless collection of 8 designs reflect how this traditional craft can be used to great effect in contemporary garment design.

Some of the designs combine knitting and crochet together, making the resulting garments more wearable and of course, fashionable.

I hope you enjoy making and wearing these garments as much as I enjoyed designing them.

Marie X

Gael

Gael

Caitlin

Keela Jacket

Keela Jacket

Finnoula

Meara

Meara

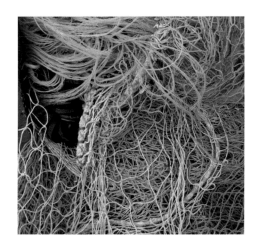

Siobhan

Siobhan

Niamh

Niamh

Catriona

Catriona

GALLERY

GAEL
Main image pages 8, 9, 10 & 11
Pattern page 43

CAITLIN
Main image pages 12, 13, 14, 15 & 39
Pattern page 40

KEELA JACKET
Main image pages 16, 17, 18 & 19
Pattern page 62

FINNOULA
Main image pages 6, 20, 21 & 74
Pattern page 50

MEARA
Main image pages 22, 23, 24 & 25
Pattern page 54

SIOBHAN
Main image pages 26, 27, 28 & 29
Pattern page 60

NIAMH
Main image pages 30, 31, 32 & 33
Pattern page 58

CATRIONA
Main image pages 34, 35, 36 & 37
Pattern page 46

CAITLIN

One size only
Rowan Felted Tweed

A	Ancient 172	2	x 50gm
B	Carbon 159	2	x 50gm
C	Delft 194	2	x 50gm
D	Celadon 184	2	x 50gm
E	Stone 190	2	x 50gm
F	Cinnamon 175	2	x 50gm
G	Barn Red 196	2	x 50gm
H	Phantom 153	2	x 50gm

Crochet hook
2.50mm (no 12) (US B1/C2) crochet hook

Tension
Based on a tension of 25 treble sts measuring 10 cm using 2.50mm (US B1/C2) crochet hook. 1 patt repeat (21 rows) measures 14 cm using 2.50mm (US B1/C2) crochet hook.

Crochet abbreviations
ch = chain; **cluster** = (yoh and insert hook as indicated for first "leg", yoh and draw loop through loosely) twice – 5 loops on hook and first "leg" of cluster completed, (yoh and insert hook as indicated for 2nd "leg", yoh and draw loop through loosely) twice – 9 loops on hook and 2nd "leg" of cluster completed, yoh and draw through 8 loops, yoh and draw through rem 2 loops on hook; **dc** = double crochet; **half cluster** = (yoh and insert hook as indicated, yoh and draw loop through loosely) twice – 5 loops on hook, yoh and draw through 4 loops, yoh and draw through rem 2 loops on hook; **sp(s)** = space(s); **ss** = slip stitch; **tr** = treble; **tr2tog** = (yoh and insert hook as indicated, yoh and draw loop through, yoh and draw through 2 loops) twice, yoh and draw through all 3 loops on hook; **yoh** = yarn over hook.

HEM BORDER STRIPE SEQUENCE
Round 1: Using yarn A.
Round 2: Using yarn B.
Round 3: Using yarn C.
Round 4: Using yarn D.
Round 5: Using yarn E.
Round 6: Using yarn F.
Round 7: Using yarn G.
Round 8: Using yarn H.
These 8 rounds form hem border stripe sequence and are repeated as required.

MAIN STRIPE SEQUENCE
Round 1: Using yarn H.
Round 2: Using yarn G.
Round 3: Using yarn F.
Round 4: Using yarn E.
Round 5: Using yarn D.
Round 6: Using yarn C.
Round 7: Using yarn B.
Round 8: Using yarn A.
These 8 rounds form main stripe sequence and are repeated throughout.

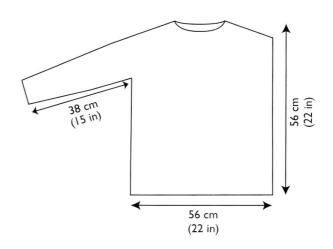

38 cm (15 in)
56 cm (22 in)
56 cm (22 in)

SLEEVES

Using 2.50mm (US B1/C2) crochet hook and yarn E, make 76 ch and join with a ss to form a ring, taking care not to twist the ch.

Foundation row (RS): 3 ch (counts as 1 tr), 1 tr into each ch to end of round. 76 sts.

Beg with **main stripe sequence** round **5** (yarn D), work in main patt as folls:

Round 1: 6 ch (counts as 1 tr and 3 ch), miss st at base of 6 ch and next 2 tr, *1 tr into each of next 2 tr, 3 ch, miss 2 tr; rep from * to last st, 1 tr into last st, ss to 3rd of 6 ch at beg of round. 19 ch sps.

Round 2: Ss into centre of first ch sp, 3 ch (counts as 1 tr), 4 tr into same ch sp, 5 tr into each ch sp to end, ss to top of 3 ch at beg of round.

Round 3: 5 ch (counts as 1 tr and 2 ch), miss st at base of 5 ch and next 3 tr, *1 tr into each of next 2 tr, 2 ch, miss 3 tr; rep from * to last st, 1 tr into last st, ss to 3rd of 5 ch at beg of round. 76 sts.

Round 4: 3 ch (counts as 1 tr), miss st at base of 3 ch, *2 tr into next ch sp**, 1 tr into each of next 2 tr; rep from * to end, ending last rep at **, 1 tr into last st, ss to top of 3 ch at beg of round.

Round 5: 3 ch (counts as 1 tr), miss st at base of 3 ch, 1 tr into each tr to end, ss to top of 3 ch at beg of round.

Round 6: 1 ch (does NOT count as st), miss st at base of 1 ch, 1 dc into each of next 2 tr, *4 ch, ss to 4th ch from hook**, 1 dc into each of next 3 tr; rep from * to end, ending last rep at **, 1 dc into last tr, ss to first tr. 25 patt reps.

Round 7: 5 ch (counts as 1 tr and 2 ch), miss (st at base of 5 ch, 1 dc, 4 ch, 1 ss and 1 dc), *1 tr into next dc, 2 ch, miss (1 dc, 4 ch, 1 ss and 1 dc); rep from * to end, ss to 3rd of 5 ch at beg of round.

Round 8: 1 ch (does NOT count as st), 1 dc into st at base of 1 ch, *(1 dc, 4 ch, ss to 4th ch from hook and 1 dc) into next ch sp, 1 dc into next tr; rep from * to end, replacing dc at end of last rep with ss to first dc.

Rounds 9 and 10: As rounds 7 and 8.

Round 11: As round 7.

Round 12: 3 ch (counts as 1 tr), miss st at base of 3 ch, 3 tr into first ch sp, 1 tr into next tr, *2 tr into next ch sp, 1 tr into next tr; rep from * to last ch sp, 3 tr into last ch sp, ss to top of 3 ch at beg of round. 77 sts.

Round 13: As round 5.

Round 14: 3 ch (counts as 1 tr), 3 tr into st at base of 3 ch, *miss 2 tr, 1 dc into next tr, miss 3 tr**, 7 tr into next tr; rep from * to end, ending last rep at **, 3 tr into same st as 3 tr at beg of round, ss to top of 3 ch at beg of round. 11 patt reps.

Round 15: 6 ch (counts as 1 tr and 3 ch), miss st at base of 6 ch and next 3 tr, *1 tr into next dc, 3 ch, miss 3 tr**, 1 tr into next tr, 3 ch, miss 3 tr; rep from * to end, ending last rep at **, ss to 3rd of 6 ch at beg of round.

Round 16: 1 ch (does NOT count as st), 1 dc into st at base of 1 ch, *3 ch, miss 3 ch, 1 dc into next st; rep from * to end, replacing dc at end of last rep with ss to first dc.

Round 17: As round 16.

Round 18: 1 ch (does NOT count as st), 1 dc into st at base of 1 ch, *miss 3 ch, 7 tr into next dc, miss 3 ch, 1 dc into next dc; rep from * to end, replacing dc at end of last rep with ss to first dc.

Round 19: 5 ch (counts as 1 tr and 2 ch), miss st at base of 5 ch and next 3 tr, *1 dc into next tr, 2 ch, miss 3 tr**, 1 tr into next dc, 2 ch, miss 3 tr;

rep from * to end, ending last rep at **, ss to 3rd of 5 ch at beg of round.

Round 20: 3 ch (counts as 1 tr), miss st at base of 3 ch, *2 tr into next ch sp, 1 tr into next st**, 3 tr into next ch sp, 1 tr into next st; rep from * to end, ending last rep at **, 2 tr into next ch sp, ss to top of 3 ch at beg of round. 76 sts.

Round 21: As round 5.

These 21 rounds form main patt.

Work in main patt for a further 33 rounds, ending after patt round 12 and a round using yarn G. (Sleeve should meas approx 37 cm.)

Fasten off.

Sleeve border

Using 2.50mm (US B1/C2) crochet hook and yarn F, with RS facing join yarn to beg of foundation ch edge of sleeve and work as folls:

1 ch (does NOT count as st), 1 dc into st at base of 1 ch, *(miss 2 sts, 5 tr into next st, miss 2 sts, 1 dc into next st) twice, miss 3 sts, 5 tr into next st, miss 2 sts, 1 dc into next st; rep from * 3 times more, replacing dc at end of last rep with ss to first dc. Fasten off.

BODY (worked in one piece)

Hem border (worked downwards)

Using 2.50mm (US B1/C2) crochet hook and yarn A, make 306 ch and join with a ss to form a ring, taking care not to twist the ch.

Foundation round (RS): 1 ch (does NOT count as st), 1 dc into ch at base of 1 ch, *miss 2 ch, 5 tr into next ch, miss 2 ch, 1 dc into next ch; rep from * to end, replacing dc at end of last rep with ss to first dc. 102 2ch spaces.

Breaking off and joining in yarns as required and beg with hem border stripe sequence round **2**, now work in stripes and border patt as folls:

Round 1: 3 ch (counts as 1 tr), 2 tr into dc at base of 3 ch, *miss 2 tr, 1 dc into next tr, 1 ch, miss (2 tr and 1 dc), 1 half cluster into next tr, (2 ch, 1 cluster into tr just worked into and next tr) 4 times, 2 ch, 1 half cluster into tr just worked into, 1 ch, miss (1 dc and 2 tr), 1 dc into next tr, miss 2 tr**, 5 tr into next dc; rep from * to end, ending last rep at **, 2 tr into same dc as tr at beg of round, ss to top of 3 ch at beg of round. 17 patt reps.

Round 2: 1 ch (does NOT count as st), 1 dc into st at base of 1 ch, *miss (2 tr, 1 dc and 1 ch), 1 half cluster into next st, (2 ch, 1 cluster into st just used and next st, missing 2 ch between these 2 sts) 5 times, 2 ch, 1 half cluster into st just worked into, miss (1 ch, 1 dc and 2 tr), 1 dc into next tr; rep from * to end, replacing dc at end of last rep with ss to first dc.

Round 3: 1 ch (does NOT count as st), 1 dc into st at base of 1 ch, *(1 dc into next st, 2 dc into next 2-ch sp) 6 times, 1 dc into each of next 2 sts; rep from * to end, replacing last dc of last rep with ss to first dc.

Round 4: 1 ch (does NOT count as st), 1 dc into st at base of 1 ch, *miss 3 dc, (5 tr into next dc, miss 2 dc, 1 dc into next dc, miss 2 dc) twice, 5 tr into next dc, miss 3 dc, 1 dc into next dc; rep from * to end, replacing dc at end of last rep with ss to first dc.

These 4 rounds form border patt.

Cont in border patt for a further 7 rounds, ending with a round using yarn D.

Next round: Using yarn F, 1 ch (does NOT count as st), 1 dc into each st

to end, ss to first dc.
Fasten off.

Main section (worked upwards)

With RS facing, using 2.50mm (US B1/C2) crochet hook and yarn H, attach yarn to foundation ch edge of hem border at beg and end of rounds and work around foundation ch edge as folls: 3 ch (counts as 1 tr), 1 tr into first 2-ch sp, 3 tr into each of next two 2-ch sps, *2 tr into next 2-ch sp, 3 tr into each of next five 2-ch sps, (2 tr into next 2-ch sp, 3 tr into each of next two 2-ch sps) twice*, rep from * to * 3 times more, 2 tr into next 2-ch sp, 3 tr into each of next two 2-ch sps, rep from * to * 4 times more, ss to top of 3 ch at beg of round. 280 sts.

Beg with main stripe sequence round **2**, now work in main patt as folls:

Round 1: 6 ch (counts as 1 tr and 3 ch), miss st at base of 6 ch and next 2 tr, *1 tr into each of next 2 tr, 3 ch, miss 2 tr; rep from * to last st, 1 tr into last st, ss to 3rd of 6 ch at beg of round. 70 ch sps.

Round 2: Ss across and into centre of first ch sp, 3 ch (counts as 1 tr), 4 tr into same ch sp, 5 tr into each ch sp to end, ss to top of 3 ch at beg of round.

Round 3: 5 ch (counts as 1 tr and 2 ch), miss st at base of 5 ch and next 3 tr, *1 tr into each of next 2 tr, 2 ch, miss 3 tr; rep from * to last st, 1 tr into last st, ss to 3rd of 5 ch at beg of round.

Round 4: 3 ch (counts as 1 tr), miss st at base of 3 ch), *2 tr into next ch sp**, 1 tr into each of next 2 tr; rep from * to end, ending last rep at **, 1 tr into last st, ss to top of 3 ch at beg of round.

Round 5: 3 ch (counts as 1 tr), miss st at base of 3 ch, 1 tr into each tr to end, ss to top of 3 ch at beg of round.

Round 6: 1 ch (does NOT count as st), miss st at base of 1 ch, 1 dc into each of next 2 tr, *4 ch, ss to 4th ch from hook**, 1 dc into each of next 3 tr; rep from * to end, ending last rep at **, 1 dc into last tr, ss to first dc. 93 patt reps.

Round 7: 5 ch (counts as 1 tr and 2 ch), miss (st at base of 5 ch, 1 dc, 4 ch, 1 ss and 1 dc), *1 tr into next dc, 2 ch, miss (1 dc, 4 ch, 1 ss and 1 dc); rep from * to end, ss to 3rd of 5 ch at beg of round.

Round 8: 1 ch (does NOT count as st), 1 dc into st at base of 1 ch, *(1 dc, 4 ch, ss to 4th ch from hook and 1 dc) into next ch sp, 1 dc into next tr; rep from * to end, replacing dc at end of last rep with ss to first dc.

Rounds 9 and 10: As rounds 7 and 8.

Round 11: As round 7.

Round 12: 3 ch (counts as 1 tr), miss st at base of 3 ch, 3 tr into first ch sp, 1 tr into next tr, *2 tr into next ch sp, 1 tr into next tr; rep from * to end, replacing tr at end of last rep with ss to top of 3 ch at beg of round. 280 sts.

Round 13: As round 5.

Round 14: 3 ch (counts as 1 tr), 3 tr into st at base of 3 ch, *miss 2 tr, 1 dc into next tr, miss 3 tr**, 7 tr into next tr; rep from * to end, ending last rep at **, 3 tr into same st as 3 tr at beg of round, ss to top of 3 ch at beg of round. 40 patt reps.

Round 15: 6 ch (counts as 1 tr and 3 ch), miss st at base of 6 ch and next 3 tr, *1 tr into next dc, 3 ch, miss 3 tr**, 1 tr into next tr, 3 ch, miss 3 tr; rep from * to end, ending last rep at **, ss to 3rd of 6 ch at beg of round.

Round 16: 1 ch (does NOT count as st), 1 dc into st at base of 1 ch, *3 ch, miss 3 ch, 1 dc into next st; rep from * to end, replacing dc at end of

last rep with ss to first dc.

Round 17: As round 16.

Round 18: 1 ch (does NOT count as st), 1 dc into st at base of 1 ch, *miss 3 ch, 7 tr into next dc, miss 3 ch, 1 dc into next dc; rep from * to end, replacing dc at end of last rep with ss to first dc.

Round 19: 5 ch (counts as 1 tr and 2 ch), miss st at base of 5 ch and next 3 tr, *1 dc into next tr, 2 ch, miss 3 tr**, 1 tr into next dc, 2 ch, miss 3 tr; rep from * to end, ending last rep at **, ss to 3rd of 5 ch at beg of round.

Round 20: 3 ch (counts as 1 tr), miss st at base of 3 ch, *3 tr into next ch sp, 1 tr into next st, 2 tr into next ch sp, 1 tr into next st; rep from * to end, replacing tr at end of last rep with ss to top of 3 ch at beg of round. 280 sts.

Round 21: As round 5.

These 21 rounds form main patt.

Work in main patt for a further 12 rounds, ending after patt round 12 and a round using yarn G. (Body should meas approx 22 cm from top of hem border.)

Shape for yoke

Keeping stripe sequence correct, shape for yoke as folls:

Next round: 3 ch (counts as 1 tr), miss st at base of 3 ch, 1 tr into each of next 69 sts, now attach first sleeve to body by working into sts of last round of sleeve, beg and ending at beg and end of sleeve rounds and working 1 tr into each of next 77 sts, 1 tr into each of next 140 sts of body, attach second sleeve to body by working into sts of last round of this sleeve, beg and ending at beg and end of sleeve rounds and working 1 tr into each of next 77 sts, 1 tr into each of last 70 sts of body, ss to top of 3 ch at beg of round. 434 sts.

Work main patt rounds 14 to 20.

Next round: 3 ch (counts as 1 tr), miss tr at base of 3 ch, 1 tr into each of next 2 tr, (tr2tog over next 2 tr, 1 tr into each of next 5 tr) 61 times, tr2tog over next 2 tr, 1 tr into each of last 2 tr, ss to top of 3 ch at beg of round. 372 sts.

Work main patt rounds 1 to 4.

Next round: 3 ch (counts as 1 tr), miss tr at base of 3 ch, 1 tr into each of next 7 tr, (tr2tog over next 2 tr, 1 tr into each of next 4 tr) 59 times, tr2tog over next 2 tr, 1 tr into each of last 8 tr, ss to top of 3 ch at beg of round. 312 sts.

Next round: 1 ch (does NOT count as st), 1 dc into st at base of 1 ch, 1 dc into next tr, *4 ch, ss to 4th ch from hook**, 1 dc into each of next 3 tr; rep from * to end, ending last rep at **, 1 dc into last tr, ss to first dc. 104 patt reps.

Work main patt rounds 7 to 11.

Next round: 3 ch (counts as 1 tr), miss st at base of 3 ch, *2 tr into next ch sp, 1 tr into next tr; rep from * to end, replacing tr at end of last rep with ss to top of 3 ch at beg of round.

Next round: 3 ch (counts as 1 tr), miss tr at base of 3 ch, 1 tr into each of next 7 tr, (tr2tog over next 2 tr, 1 tr into each of next 3 tr) 59 times, tr2tog over next 2 tr, 1 tr into each of last 7 tr, ss to top of 3 ch at beg of round. 252 sts.

Work main patt rounds 14 to 20.

Next round: 3 ch (counts as 1 tr), miss tr at base of 3 ch, 1 tr into each of next 6 tr, (tr2tog over next 2 tr, 1 tr into each of next 2 tr) 59 times,

tr2tog over next 2 tr, 1 tr into each of last 7 tr, ss to top of 3 ch at beg of round. 192 sts.
Work main patt rounds 1 to 4.
Next round: 3 ch (counts as 1 tr), miss tr at base of 3 ch, 1 tr into each of next 6 tr, (tr2tog over next 2 tr, 1 tr into next tr) 59 times, tr2tog over next 2 tr, 1 tr into each of last 6 tr, ss to top of 3 ch at beg of round, turn. 132 sts.
Next round: 1 ch (does NOT count as st), 1 dc into st at base of 1 ch, 1 dc into next dc, *4 ch, ss to 4th ch from hook**, 1 dc into each of next 3 dc, rep from * to end, ending last rep at **, 1 dc into last dc, ss to first

dc. 44 patt reps.
Work main patt rounds 7 to 9.
Next round: 3 ch (counts as 1 tr), miss st at base of 3 ch, *2 tr into next ch sp, 1 tr into next tr; rep from * to end, replacing tr at end of last rep with ss to top of 3 ch at beg of round. 132 sts.
Fasten off.

MAKING UP
Press as described on the information page.
See information page for finishing instructions.

GAEL

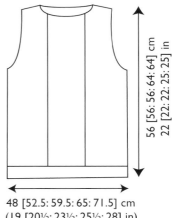

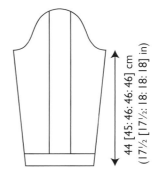

56 [56: 56: 64: 64] cm
22 [22: 22: 25: 25] in

48 [52.5: 59.5: 65: 71.5] cm
(19 [20½: 23½: 25½: 28] in)

44 [45: 46: 46: 46] cm
(17½ [17½: 18: 18: 18] in)

Needles and crochet hook
1 pair 2¾mm (no 12) (US 2) needles
1 pair 3mm (no 11) (US 2/3) needles
2.50mm (no 12) (US B1/C2) crochet hook

	S	M	L	XL	XXL	
To fit bust	81-86	91-97	102-107	112-117	122-127	cm
	32-34	36-38	40-42	44-46	48-50	in
Rowan Felted Tweed						
	7	8	8	10	11	× 50gm

(photographed in Delft 194)

Tension

25 sts and 36 rows to 10 cm measured over st st using 3mm (US 2/3) needles. Crochet motif is 8 cm square using 2.50mm (US B1/C2) crochet hook.

Crochet abbreviations

ch = chain; **dc** = double crochet; **dtr** = double treble; **dtr2tog** = *(yoh) twice and insert hook as indicated, yoh and draw loop through, (yoh and draw through 2 loops) twice; rep from * once more, yoh and draw through all 3 loops on hook; **dtr3tog** = *(yoh) twice and insert hook as indicated, yoh and draw loop through, (yoh and draw through 2 loops) twice; rep from * twice more, yoh and draw through all 4 loops on hook; **picot** = 5 ch, 1 ss into 5th ch from hook; **qntr** = quintuple treble; **sp(s)** = space(s); **ss** = slip stitch; **yoh** = yarn over hook.

BASIC CROCHET MOTIF

Using 2.50mm (US B1/C2) crochet hook, work as folls:
Round 1 (RS): (5 ch, dtr3tog into 5th ch from hook) 4 times, ss to ch at base of first dtr3tog to form a ring.
Round 1 forms a ring made up of 4 groups of sts – when working round 2, work the sts of this round into the point where these groups join at the base of a dtr3tog.
Round 2: 1 ch (does NOT count as st), 1 dc into same place as ss at end of previous round, *5 ch, 1 picot, 5 ch, (1 dc, 13 ch and 1 dc) into next point where groups of sts join; rep from * twice more, 5 ch, 1 picot, 5 ch, (1 dc, 6 ch and 1 qntr) into same place as dc at beg of round.
Round 3: 4 ch (does NOT count as st), (dtr2tog, 3 ch and dtr3tog) into ch sp partly formed by qntr at end of previous round, *3 ch, 1 dtr into ch before picot along next ch sp, 3 ch, 1 dtr into ch after picot along same ch sp, 3 ch*, (dtr3tog, 3 ch, dtr3tog, 3 ch, dtr3tog, 3 ch and dtr3tog) into next 13-ch sp; rep from * to end, ending last rep at **, (dtr3tog, 3 ch and dtr3tog) into same ch sp as used at beg of round, 3 ch, ss to top of dtr2tog at beg of round.
Completed motif is a square shape. In each corner there are four drt3tog (clusters), and at centre of each side there are 2 dtr (one at each side of the picot of round 2). There is a 3-ch sp in each corner and a further five 3-ch sps between these corner ch sps. Join motifs whilst working round 3 by replacing the "3 ch" of each corner 3-ch sp and the 3-ch sp above the picot with "1 ch, 1 ss into corresponding ch sp of adjacent motif, 1 ch".

BACK and FRONT (both alike)

Motif panel

Make and join 6 [6: 6: 7: 7] motifs to form a strip 1 motif wide and 6 [6: 6: 7: 7] motifs long.
Make a further strip in the same way.

Join strips

With RS of motifs tog and using 2.50mm (US B1/C2) crochet hook, join the two motif strips along one long edge matching all the chain spaces and clusters tog. Join yarn to one end and work along the row as folls:
1 ch (does NOT count as st), work 1 dc into each corner 3-ch sp, 1 dc into each cluster and 3 dc into each 3-ch sp of each motif to end of row.
Fasten off.

With RS facing and using 2.50mm (US B1/C2) crochet hook, attach yarn to one corner 3-ch sp of joined motif panel and work edging row along one long edge of motifs as folls:
Edging row (RS): 1 ch (does NOT count as st), 3 dc into same corner 3-ch sp, *3 dc into each of next five 3-ch sps**, 2 dc into next corner 3-ch sp, 1 dc over joining point between motifs, 2 dc into corner 3-ch sp of next motif; rep from * to end, ending last rep at **, 2 dc into last corner 3-ch sp. 120 [120: 120: 140: 140] sts.
Fasten off.
Work edging row along other side of joined motif panel in same way.

First side panel

(This panel is left side panel for back, or right side panel for front.)
With RS facing and using 3mm (US 2/3) needles, pick up and knit 120 [120: 120: 140: 140] sts evenly along one side of motif panel. (This is 1 st for every dc of edging row.)
Beg with a P row, work in st st throughout as folls:
Work 1 [1: 3: 3: 5] rows, ending with RS facing for next row.
Inc 1 st at beg of next and foll alt row, then at same edge on foll 3 rows, ending with RS facing for next row. 125 [125: 125: 145: 145] sts.
Place marker at end of last row – this denotes neck shoulder point.

Shape shoulder seam

Work 3 [3: 4: 4: 4] rows, ending with **WS** [**WS**: RS: RS: RS] facing for next row.
Dec 1 st at marked end of next row and at same (shoulder) edge of 1 [5: 7: 4: 7] foll 4th [4th: 4th: 5th: 5th] rows, then at same edge on 6 [2: -: 3: -] foll 3rd [3rd: -: 4th: -] rows. 117 [117: 117: 137: 137] sts.
Work 2 [2: 3: 3: 4] rows, ending with RS facing for next row.

Shape armhole

Cast off 30 [32: 31: 31: 30] sts at beg of next row, then 4 sts at beg of foll alt row. 83 [81: 82: 102: 103] sts.
Dec 1 st at shaped edge of next 8 [8: 10: 12: 14] rows, then on foll 3 [4: 5: 6: 7] alt rows. 72 [69: 67: 84: 82] sts.
Work 5 [7: 9: 11: 13] rows, ending with RS facing for next row.
Cast off. (This cast-off edge forms side seam.)

Second side panel

(This panel is right side panel for back, or left side panel for front.)
With RS facing and using 3mm (US 2/3) needles, pick up and knit 120 [120: 120: 140: 140] sts evenly along other side of motif panel.
Beg with a P row, work in st st throughout as folls:
Work 1 [1: 3: 3: 5] rows, ending with RS facing for next row.
Inc 1 st at end of next and foll alt row, then at same edge on foll 3 rows, ending with RS facing for next row. 125 [125: 125: 145: 145] sts.
Place marker at beg of last row – this denotes neck shoulder point.
Complete to match first side panel, reversing shapings.

Hem border

With RS facing and using 2.50mm (US B1/C2) crochet hook, attach yarn at base of one side seam and work edging row along lower edge of side and motif panels as folls:
Edging row (RS): 1 ch (does NOT count as st), work 38 [44: 53: 59: 68] dc along lower row-end edge of first side panel, 1 dc into edging row along side of motif panel, 2 dc into corner 3-ch sp of motif, *3 dc into each of next five 3-ch sps, 2 dc into next corner 3-ch sp**, 1 dc over joining point between motifs, 2 dc into corner 3-ch sp of next motif, rep from * to **

once more, 1 dc into edging row along side of motif panel, work 38 [44: 53: 59: 68] dc along lower row-end edge of second side panel. 117 [129: 147: 159: 177] sts.

Fasten off.

With RS facing and using 2¾mm (US 2) needles, pick up and knit 117 [129: 147: 159: 177] sts evenly along top of edging row. (This is 1 st for every dc of edging row.)

Row 1 (WS): P3, *K3, P3, rep from * to end.

Row 2: K3, *P3, K3, rep from * to end.

These 2 rows form rib.

Cont in rib until hem border meas 6 cm from edge of motif and side panels, ending with RS facing for next row.

Cast off in rib.

SLEEVES

Motif panel

Make and join 6 motifs to form one strip of 6 motifs.

With RS facing and using 2.50mm (US B1/C2) crochet hook, attach yarn to one corner 3-ch sp of joined motif strip and work edging row along one long edge of motif strip as folls:

Edging row (RS): 1 ch (does NOT count as st), 3 dc into same corner 3-ch sp, *3 dc into each of next five 3-ch sps**, 2 dc into next corner 3-ch sp, 1 dc over joining point between motifs, 2 dc into corner 3-ch sp of next motif; rep from * to end, ending last rep at **, 2 dc into last corner 3-ch sp. 120 sts.

Fasten off.

Work edging row along other side of motif strip in same way.

First side section

With RS facing and using 3mm (US 2/3) needles, pick up and knit 120 sts evenly along one side of motif strip. (This is 1 st for every dc of edging row.)

Beg with a P row, work in st st throughout as folls:

Work 3 rows, ending with RS facing for next row.

Dec 1 st at end of next and foll 6 [7: 7: 7: 8] alt rows.

113 [112: 112: 112: 111] sts.

Work 1 row, ending with RS facing for next row.

Shape sleeve seam

Cast off 5 sts at beg of next and foll 1 [2: 10: 17: 17] alt rows, then 6 [6: 6: -: -] sts at beg of foll 14 [13: 6: -: -] alt rows **and at same time** dec 1 st at end of next and foll 12 [12: 14: 15: 15] alt rows. 6 [6: 6: 6: 5] sts.

Work 1 row, ending with RS facing for next row.

Cast off rem 6 [6: 6: 6: 5] sts.

Second side section

With RS facing and using 3mm (US 2/3) needles, pick up and knit 120 sts evenly along other side of motif strip.

Beg with a P row, work in st st throughout as folls:

Work 3 rows, ending with RS facing for next row.

Dec 1 st at beg of next and foll 6 [7: 7: 7: 8] alt rows.

113 [112: 112: 112: 111] sts.

Complete to match first side section, reversing shapings.

Cuff border

With RS facing and using 2.50mm (US B1/C2) crochet hook, attach yarn at base of sleeve seam and work edging row along lower edge of side

sections and motif strip as folls:

Edging row (RS): 1 ch (does NOT count as st), work 12 [13: 15: 15: 16] dc along lower row-end edge of first side section, 1 dc into edging row along side of motif strip, 2 dc into corner 3-ch sp of motif, 3 dc into each of next five 3-ch sps, 2 dc into next corner 3-ch sp, 1 dc into edging row along side of motif strip, work 12 [13: 15: 15: 16] dc along lower row-end edge of second side section. 45 [47: 51: 51: 53] sts.

Fasten off.

With RS facing and using 2¾mm (US 2) needles, pick up and knit 45 [47: 51: 51: 53] sts evenly along top of last row. (This is 1 st for every dc of edging row.)

Row 1 (WS): K0 [1: 0: 0: 1], P3, *K3, P3, rep from * to last 0 [1: 0: 0: 1] sts, K0 [1: 0: 0: 1].

Row 2: P0 [1: 0: 0: 1], K3, *P3, K3, rep from * to last 0 [1: 0: 0: 1] sts, P0 [1: 0: 0: 1].

These 2 rows form rib.

Cont in rib until cuff border meas 4 [5: 7: 7.5: 8] cm from edge of motif and side sections, ending with RS facing for next row.

Cast off in rib.

MAKING UP

Press as described on the information page.

Join right shoulder seam using back stitch, or mattress stitch if preferred.

Neckband

With RS facing and using 2.50mm (US B1/C2) crochet hook, attach yarn at left shoulder neck point and work edging row around entire neck edge as folls:

Edging row (RS): 1 ch (does NOT count as st), work 7 [7: 9: 9: 10] dc down left side of front neck, 1 dc into edging row along side of motif panel, 2 dc into corner 3-ch sp of motif, *3 dc into each of next five 3-ch sps, 2 dc into next corner 3-ch sp**, 1 dc over joining point between motifs, 2 dc into corner 3-ch sp of next motif, rep from * to ** once more, 1 dc into edging row along side of motif panel, 7 [7: 8: 8: 10] dc up right side of front neck, 7 [7: 9: 9: 10] dc down right side of back neck, 1 dc into edging row along side of motif panel, 2 dc into corner 3-ch sp of motif, ***3 dc into each of next five 3-ch sps, 2 dc into next corner 3-ch sp****, 1 dc over joining point between motifs, rep from *** to **** once more, 1 dc into edging row along side of motif panel, and 8 [8: 9: 9: 11] dc up left side of back neck.

111 [111: 117: 117: 123] sts.

Fasten off.

With RS facing and using 2¾mm (US 2) needles, pick up and knit 111 [111: 117: 117: 123] sts evenly along top of last row. (This is 1 st for every dc of edging row.)

Beg with row 1, work in rib as given for rib section of hem border of back and front for 2 cm, ending with RS facing for next row.

Cast off in rib.

Join left shoulder and neckband seam. Join side seams. Join sleeve seams.

Insert sleeves into armholes.

See information page for finishing instructions.

CATRIONA

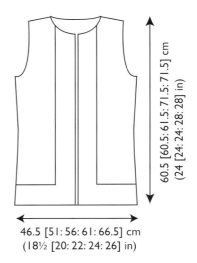

BODY (worked in one piece to armholes)
Knitted section
Using 3mm (US 2/3) needles and yarn A cast on 202 [226: 250: 274: 302] sts. (**Note**: Due to the number of sts, you may prefer to work using a circular needle.)

Beg with a K row, work in st st throughout as folls:

Work straight until body meas 4 [3: 3: 13: 13] cm, ending with RS facing for next row.

Counting in from both ends of last row, place side seam markers after 43rd [49th: 55th: 61st: 68th] st in from both ends of row.

Next row (RS): *K to within 4 sts of side seam marker, sl 1, K1, psso, K4 (marker is at centre of these 4 sts), K2tog; rep from * once more, K to end.

Working all decreases near side seam markers as set by last row, dec 1 st near each side seam marker on 8th and 3 foll 6th rows.
182 [206: 230: 254: 282] sts.

●●●

	S	M	L	XL	XXL	
To fit bust	81-86	91-97	102-107	112-117	122-127	cm
	32-34	36-38	40-42	44-46	48-50	in
Rowan Felted Tweed						
A Barn Red 196	6	6	7	8	9	× 50gm
B Cinnamon 175	2	2	3	3	3	× 50gm

60.5 [60.5: 61.5: 71.5: 71.5] cm (24 [24: 24: 28: 28] in)

46.5 [51: 56: 61: 66.5] cm (18½ [20: 22: 24: 26] in)

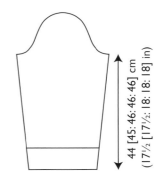

44 [45: 46: 46: 46] cm (17½ [17½: 18: 18: 18] in)

Needles and crochet hook
1 pair 2¾mm (no 12) (US 2) needles
1 pair 3mm (no 11) (US 2/3) needles
2.50mm (no 12) (US B1/C2) crochet hook

Buttons – 7 x BN1116 from Bedecked – see information page for details.

Tension
25 sts and 36 rows to 10 cm measured over st st using 3mm (US 2/3) needles.

Crochet abbreviations
ch = chain; **dc** = double crochet; **dtr** = double treble; **htr** = half treble; **picot** = 3 ch, 1 ss into 3rd ch from hook; **qtr** = quadruple treble; **sp(s)** = space(s); **ss** = slip stitch; **tr** = treble; **tr3tog** = (yoh and insert hook as indicated, yoh and draw loop through, yoh and draw through 2 loops) 3 times, yoh and draw through all 4 loops on hook; **yoh** = yarn over hook.

Work 17 rows, ending with RS facing for next row.

Next row (RS): *K to within 2 sts of side seam marker, M1, K4 (marker is at centre of these 4 sts), M1, rep from * once more, K to end.

Working all increases near side seam markers as set by last row, inc 1 st near each side seam marker on 10th and 3 foll 10th rows.
202 [226: 250: 274: 302] sts.

Cont straight until body meas 32 [31: 31: 40: 39] cm, ending with RS facing for next row.

Divide for armholes

Next row (RS): K38 [43: 48: 53: 59] and slip these sts onto a holder (for right front), cast off next 10 [12: 14: 16: 18] sts, K until there are 106 [116: 126: 136: 148] sts on right needle and turn, leaving rem 48 [55: 62: 69: 77] sts on another holder (for left front).

Shape back

Work on centre set of 106 [116: 126: 136: 148] sts only for back as folls:
Work 1 row, ending with RS facing for next row.
Dec 1 st at each end of next 5 [7: 7: 9: 9] rows, then on foll 5 [6: 7: 6: 8] alt rows. 86 [90: 98: 106: 114] sts.

Cont straight until back meas 18 [19: 20: 21: 22] cm from dividing row, ending with RS facing for next row.

Shape shoulders

Cast off 3 [3: 4: 4: 5] sts at beg of next 2 rows. 80 [84: 90: 98: 104] sts.

Shape back neck

Next row (RS): Cast off 3 [3: 4: 5: 5] sts, K until there are 20 [22: 23: 26: 28] sts on right needle and turn, leaving rem sts on a holder.
Work each side of neck separately.
Dec 1 st at neck edge of next 6 rows **and at same time** cast off 3 [4: 4: 5: 5] sts at beg of 2nd and foll 1 [2: 2: 2: 1] alt rows, and 4 [-: -: -: 6] sts at beg of foll 1 [-: -: -: 1] alt row.
Work 1 row.
Cast off rem 4 [4: 5: 5: 6] sts.
With RS facing, slip centre 34 [34: 36: 36: 38] sts onto another holder (for neckband), rejoin yarn and K to end.
Complete to match first side, reversing shapings.

Shape left front

With RS facing, rejoin yarn to 48 [55: 62: 69: 77] sts on left front holder, cast off 10 [12: 14: 16: 18] sts, K to end.
Work on this set of 38 [43: 48: 53: 59] sts for left front as folls:
Work 1 row, ending with RS facing for next row.
Dec 1 st at armhole edge of next 5 [7: 7: 9: 9] rows, then on foll 5 [6: 7: 6: 8] alt rows. 28 [30: 34: 38: 42] sts.
Cont straight until 18 [18: 22: 22: 26] rows less have been worked than on back to beg of shoulder shaping, ending with RS facing for next row.

Shape front neck

Place marker at front opening edge of next row (to denote beg of front neck shaping).
Dec 1 st at marked edge of next 3 rows, then on foll alt row, then on 3 [3: 4: 4: 5] foll 4th rows. 21 [23: 26: 30: 33] sts.
Work 1 row, ending with RS facing for next row.

Shape shoulder

Cast off 3 [3: 4: 4: 5] sts at beg of next and foll 3 [1: 4: 0: 3] alt rows, then

4 [4: -: 5: 6] sts at beg of foll 1 [3: -: 4: 1] alt rows **and at same time** dec 1 st at neck edge of 3rd row.
Work 1 row.
Cast off rem 4 [4: 5: 5: 6] sts.

Shape right front

With **WS** facing, rejoin yarn to 38 [43: 48: 53: 59] sts on right front holder and P to end.
Complete to match left front, reversing shapings.

Crochet trim

With RS facing, using 2.50mm (US B1/C2) crochet hook and yarn B, attach yarn at marked (beg of front neck shaping) point along left front opening edge, 1 ch (does NOT count as st), work 116 [116: 116: 142: 142] dc evenly down left front opening edge to cast-on edge, 1 dc into corner at base of front opening edge (place marker on this dc), 205 [231: 257: 283: 309] dc along entire cast-on edge, 1 dc into corner at base of right front opening edge (place marker on this dc), then 116 [116: 116: 142: 142] dc evenly up right front opening edge to marked (beg of front neck shaping) point, turn. 439 [465: 491: 569: 595] sts.

Row 1 (WS): 4 ch (counts as 1 tr and 1 ch), miss first 2 dc, 1 tr into next dc, *1 ch, miss 1 dc, 1 tr into next dc; rep from * to end, working (1 tr, 3 ch and 1 tr) into each marked corner dc, turn.

Row 2: 1 ch (does NOT count as st), 1 dc into tr at base of 1 ch, (1 dc into next ch sp, 1 dc into next tr) 3 times, 2 ch, miss 1 ch, 1 htr into next tr, 2 ch, miss (1 ch, 1 tr, 1 ch and 1 tr), (tr3tog, 2 ch, tr3tog, 2 ch, tr3tog, 2 ch and tr3tog) into next ch sp, 2 ch, miss (1 tr, 1 ch, 1 tr and 1 ch), 1 htr into next tr, 2 ch, miss 1 ch, (1 dc into next tr, 1 dc into next ch sp) 3 times, **1 dc into next tr, (1 dc into next ch sp, 1 dc into next tr) 3 times, 2 ch, miss 1 ch, 1 htr into next tr, 2 ch, miss (1 ch, 1 tr, 1 ch and 1 tr), (tr3tog, 2 ch, tr3tog, 2 ch and tr3tog) into next ch sp, 2 ch, miss (1 tr, 1 ch, 1 tr and 1 ch), 1 htr into next tr, 2 ch, miss 1 ch, (1 dc into next tr, 1 dc into next ch sp) 3 times**, rep from ** to ** 2 [2: 2: 3: 3] times more, ***1 dc into next tr, (1 dc into next ch sp, 1 dc into next tr) 3 times, 2 ch, miss 1 ch, 1 htr into next tr, 2 ch, miss (1 ch, 1 tr, 1 ch and 1 tr), (tr3tog, 2 ch, tr3tog, 2 ch, tr3tog, 2 ch, tr3tog, 2 ch and tr3tog) into next (corner) ch sp, 2 ch, miss (1 tr, 1 ch, 1 tr and 1 ch), 1 htr into next tr, 2 ch, miss 1 ch, (1 dc into next tr, 1 dc into next ch sp) 3 times***, rep from ** to ** 7 [8: 9: 10: 11] times more, rep from *** to *** once more, rep from ** to ** 4 [4: 4: 5: 5] times more, 1 dc into top of 3rd of 4 ch at beg of previous row, turn. 17 [18: 19: 22: 23] patt reps of which 2 reps are corner reps.

Row 3: 1 ch (does NOT count as st), 1 dc into each of first 5 dc, 3 ch, miss (2 dc and 2 ch), 1 tr into next htr, 3 ch, miss 2 ch, 1 tr into next tr3tog, 1 picot, miss 2 ch, 1 tr into next tr3tog, 1 ch, 1 picot, 1 ch, miss 2 ch, 1 tr into next tr3tog, 1 picot, miss 2 ch, 1 tr into next tr3tog, 3 ch, miss 2 ch, 1 tr into next htr, 3 ch, miss (2 ch and 2 dc), 1 dc into each of next 4 dc, **1 dc into each of next 5 dc, 3 ch, miss (2 dc and 2 ch), 1 tr into next htr, 3 ch, miss 2 ch, 1 tr into next tr3tog, 1 picot, miss 2 ch, 1 tr into next tr3tog, 1 ch, 1 picot, 1 ch, miss 2 ch, 1 tr into next tr3tog, 1 picot, miss 2 ch, 1 tr into next tr3tog, 3 ch, miss 2 ch, 1 tr into next htr, 3 ch, miss (2 ch and 2 dc), 1 dc into each of next 4 dc**, rep from ** to ** 2 [2: 2: 3: 3] times more, ***1 dc into each of next 5 dc, 3 ch, miss (2 dc and 2 ch), 1 tr into next htr, (3 ch, miss 2 ch, 1 tr into next tr3tog) twice,

(1 ch, 1 picot, 1 ch, miss 2 ch, 1 tr into next tr3tog) 3 times, 3 ch, miss 2 ch, 1 tr into next tr3tog, 3 ch, miss 2 ch, 1 tr into next htr, 3 ch, miss (2 ch and 2 dc), 1 dc into each of next 4 dc***, rep from ** to ** 7 [8: 9: 10: 11] times more, rep from *** to *** once more, rep from ** to ** 4 [4: 4: 5: 5] times more, 1 dc into last dc, turn.

Row 4: 1 ch (does NOT count as st), 1 dc into each of first 3 dc, 4 ch, miss (2 dc and 3 ch), 1 tr into next tr, 6 ch, miss 3 ch, 1 tr into next tr, 4 ch, miss 1 picot, 1 tr into next tr, 6 ch, miss (1 ch, 1 picot and 1 ch), 1 tr into next tr, 4 ch, miss 1 picot, 1 tr into next tr, 6 ch, miss 3 ch, 1 tr into next tr, 4 ch, miss (3 ch and 2 dc), 1 dc into each of next 2 dc, **1 dc into each of next 3 dc, 4 ch, miss (2 dc and 3 ch), 1 tr into next tr, 6 ch, miss 3 ch, 1 tr into next tr, 4 ch, miss 1 picot, 1 tr into next tr, 6 ch, miss (1 ch, 1 picot and 1 ch), 1 tr into next tr, 4 ch, miss 1 picot, 1 tr into next tr, 6 ch, miss 3 ch, 1 tr into next tr, 4 ch, miss (3 ch and 2 dc), 1 dc into each of next 2 dc**, rep from ** to ** 2 [2: 2: 3: 3] times more, ***1 dc into each of next 3 dc, 4 ch, miss (2 dc and 3 ch), 1 tr into next tr, 6 ch, miss 3 ch, 1 tr into next tr, 4 ch, miss 3 ch, 1 tr into next tr, 6 ch, miss (1 ch, 1 picot and 1 ch), 1 tr into next tr, 4 ch, miss (1 ch, 1 picot and 1 ch), 1 tr into next tr, 6 ch, miss (1 ch, 1 picot and 1 ch), 1 tr into next tr, 4 ch, miss 3 ch, 1 tr into next tr, 6 ch, miss 3 ch, 1 tr into next tr, 4 ch, miss (3 ch and 2 dc), 1 dc into each of next 2 dc***, rep from ** to ** 7 [8: 9: 10: 11] times more, rep from *** to *** once more, rep from ** to ** 4 [4: 4: 5: 5] times more, 1 dc into last dc, turn.

Row 5: 1 ch (does NOT count as st), 1 dc into each of first 2 dc, miss 1 dc, (5 dc into next 4-ch sp, 7 dc into next 6-ch sp) 3 times, 5 dc into next 4-ch sp, miss 1 dc, 1 dc into next dc, **1 dc into each of next 2 dc, miss 1 dc, (5 dc into next 4-ch sp, 7 dc into next 6-ch sp) 3 times, 5 dc into next 4-ch sp, miss 1 dc, 1 dc into next dc**, rep from ** to ** 2 [2: 2: 3: 3] times more, ***1 dc into each of next 2 dc, miss 1 dc, (5 dc into next 4-ch sp, 7 dc into next 6-ch sp) 4 times, 5 dc into next 4-ch sp, miss 1 dc, 1 dc into next dc***, rep from ** to ** 7 [8: 9: 10: 11] times more, rep from *** to *** once more, rep from ** to ** 4 [4: 4: 5: 5] times more, 1 dc into last dc, turn.

Row 6: 1 ch (does NOT count as st), 1 dc into first dc, 1 ch, miss 3 dc, 1 dc into next dc, 2 ch, miss 2 dc, 1 tr into next dc, (1 picot, miss 1 dc, 1 tr into next dc) 3 times, 2 ch, miss 2 dc, 1 dc into next dc, 2 ch, miss 2 dc, 1 tr into next dc, (1 picot, miss 1 dc, 1 tr into next dc) 3 times, 2 ch, miss 2 dc, 1 dc into next dc, 2 ch, miss 2 dc, 1 tr into next dc, (1 picot, miss 1 dc, 1 tr into next dc) 3 times, 2 ch, miss 2 dc, 1 dc into next dc, 1 ch, miss 3 dc, **miss 4 dc, 1 dc into next dc, 2 ch, miss 2 dc, 1 tr into next dc, (1 picot, miss 1 dc, 1 tr into next dc) 3 times, 2 ch, miss 2 dc, 1 dc into next dc, 2 ch, miss 2 dc, 1 tr into next dc, (1 picot, miss 1 dc, 1 tr into next dc) 3 times, 2 ch, miss 2 dc, 1 dc into next dc, 2 ch, miss 2 dc, 1 tr into next dc, (1 picot, miss 1 dc, 1 tr into next dc) 3 times, 2 ch, miss 2 dc, 1 dc into next dc, 1 ch, miss 3 dc**, rep from ** to ** 2 [2: 2: 3: 3] times more, ***miss 4 dc, 1 dc into next dc, 2 ch, miss 2 dc, 1 tr into next dc, (1 picot, miss 1 dc, 1 tr into next dc) 3 times, 2 ch, miss 2 dc, 1 dc into next dc, 2 ch, miss 2 dc, 1 tr into next dc, (1 picot, miss 1 dc, 1 tr into next dc) 9 times, 2 ch, miss 2 dc, 1 dc into next dc, 2 ch, miss 2 dc, 1 tr into next dc, (1 picot, miss 1 dc, 1 tr into next dc) 3 times, 2 ch, miss 2 dc, 1 dc into next dc, 1 ch, miss 3 dc***, rep from ** to ** 7 [8: 9: 10: 11] times more, rep from *** to *** once more, rep from ** to ** 4 [4: 4: 5: 5]

times more, 1 dc into last dc, turn.

Row 7: 6 ch (counts as 1 qtr), 1 dtr into first picot, 3 ch, 1 tr into next picot, 2 ch, 1 htr into next picot, 3 ch, 1 dc into next picot, 2 ch, 1 ss into next picot, 2 ch, 1 dc into next picot, 3 ch, 1 htr into next picot, 2 ch, 1 tr into next picot, 2 ch, 1 dtr into next picot, **miss 1 ch sp, 1 qtr into next ch sp (the ch sp lying above 7 dc of row 5), 1 dtr into next picot, 3 ch, 1 tr into next picot, 2 ch, 1 htr into next picot, 3 ch, 1 dc into next picot, 2 ch, 1 ss into next picot, 2 ch, 1 dc into next picot, 3 ch, 1 htr into next picot, 2 ch, 1 tr into next picot, 2 ch, 1 dtr into next picot**, rep from ** to ** 2 [2: 2: 3: 3] times more, ***miss 1 ch sp, 1 qtr into next ch sp (the ch sp lying above 7 dc of row 5), 1 dtr into next picot, 3 ch, 1 tr into next picot, 2 ch, 1 htr into next picot, 3 ch, 1 dc into next picot, 2 ch, 1 ss into next picot, 2 ch, 1 dc into next picot, 2 ch, 1 htr into next picot, 2 ch, 1 tr into next picot (mark this corner tr), 2 ch, 1 htr into next picot, 2 ch, 1 dc into next picot, 2 ch, 1 ss into next picot, 2 ch, 1 dc into next picot, 3 ch, 1 htr into next picot, 2 ch, 1 tr into next picot, 3 ch, 1 dtr into next picot***, rep from ** to ** 7 [8: 9: 10: 11] times more, rep from *** to *** once more, rep from ** to ** 4 [4: 4: 5: 5] times more, 1 qtr into last dc, turn.

Row 8: 1 ch (does NOT count as st), 1 dc into each st to end, working 3 dc into each marked corner tr.
Fasten off.

SLEEVES
Knitted section
Using 3mm (US 2/3) needles and yarn A cast on 50 [50: 54: 54: 58] sts.
Beg with a K row, work in st st throughout as folls:
Inc 1 st at each end of 5th [3rd: 5th: 3rd: 3rd] and every foll 6th [6th: 6th: 4th: 4th] row to 80 [90: 94: 66: 70] sts, then on every foll 8th [-: -: 6th: 6th] row until there are 86 [-: -: 98: 102] sts.
Cont straight until sleeve meas 36.5 [37.5: 38.5: 38.5: 38.5] cm, ending with RS facing for next row.
Shape top
Cast off 5 [6: 7: 8: 9] sts at beg of next 2 rows. 76 [78: 80: 82: 84] sts.
Dec 1 st at each end of next 5 rows, then on foll 4 alt rows, then on 4 foll 4th rows. 50 [52: 54: 56: 58] sts.
Work 1 row.
Dec 1 st at each end of next and every foll alt row to 40 sts, then on foll 7 rows, ending with RS facing for next row. 26 sts.
Cast off 4 sts at beg of next 2 rows.
Cast off rem 18 sts.
Crochet trim
With RS facing, using 2.50mm (US B1/C2) crochet hook and yarn B, attach yarn to one end of cast-on edge, 1 ch (does NOT count as st), work 53 [53: 57: 57: 61] dc evenly across entire cast-on edge, turn. 53 [53: 57: 57: 61] sts.
Row 1 (WS): 4 ch (counts as 1 tr and 1 ch), miss first 2 dc, 1 tr into next dc, *1 ch, miss 1 dc, 1 tr into next dc; rep from * to end, turn.
Row 2: 1 ch (does NOT count as st), 1 dc into tr at base of 1 ch, (1 dc into next ch sp, 1 dc into next tr) 3 [3: 4: 4: 5] times, 2 ch, miss 1 ch, 1 htr into next tr, 2 ch, miss (1 ch, 1 tr, 1 ch and 1 tr), (tr3tog, 2 ch, tr3tog, 2 ch, tr3tog, 2 ch and tr3tog) into next ch sp, 2 ch, miss (1 tr, 1 ch, 1 tr and 1 ch), 1 htr into next tr, 2 ch, miss 1 ch, (1 dc into next tr, 1 dc into next ch

sp) 3 times, I dc into next tr, (I dc into next ch sp, I dc into next tr) 3 times, 2 ch, miss I ch, I htr into next tr, 2 ch, miss (I ch, I tr, I ch and I tr), (tr3tog, 2 ch, tr3tog, 2 ch, tr3tog, 2 ch and tr3tog) into next ch sp, 2 ch, miss (I tr, I ch, I tr and I ch), I htr into next tr, 2 ch, miss I ch, (I dc into next tr, I dc into next ch sp) 3 [3: 4: 4: 5] times, I dc into 3rd of 4 ch at beg of previous row, turn. 2 patt reps plus 0 [0: 2: 2: 4] sts at each end.

Row 3: I ch (does NOT count as st), I dc into each of first 5 [5: 7: 7: 9] dc, 3 ch, miss (2 dc and 2 ch), I tr into next htr, 3 ch, miss 2 ch, I tr into next tr3tog, I picot, miss 2 ch, I tr into next tr3tog, I ch, I picot, I ch, miss 2 ch, I tr into next tr3tog, I picot, miss 2 ch, I tr into next tr3tog, 3 ch, miss 2 ch, I tr into next htr, 3 ch, miss (2 ch and 2 dc), I dc into each of next 9 dc, 3 ch, miss (2 dc and 2 ch), I tr into next htr, 3 ch, miss 2 ch, I tr into next tr3tog, I picot, miss 2 ch, I tr into next tr3tog, I ch, I picot, I ch, miss 2 ch, I tr into next tr3tog, I picot, miss 2 ch, I tr into next tr3tog, 3 ch, miss 2 ch, I tr into next htr, 3 ch, miss (2 ch and 2 dc), I dc into each of last 5 [5: 7: 7: 9] dc, turn.

Row 4: I ch (does NOT count as st), I dc into each of first 3 [3: 5: 5: 7] dc, 4 ch, miss (2 dc and 3 ch), I tr into next tr, 6 ch, miss 3 ch, I tr into next tr, 4 ch, miss I picot, I tr into next tr, 6 ch, miss (I ch, I picot and I ch), I tr into next tr, 4 ch, miss I picot, I tr into next tr, 6 ch, miss 3 ch, I tr into next tr, 4 ch, miss (3 ch and 2 dc), I dc into each of next 5 dc, 4 ch, miss (2 dc and 3 ch), I tr into next tr, 6 ch, miss 3 ch, I tr into next tr, 4 ch, miss I picot, I tr into next tr, 6 ch, miss (I ch, I picot and I ch), I tr into next tr, 4 ch, miss I picot, I tr into next tr, 6 ch, miss 3 ch, I tr into next tr, 4 ch, miss (3 ch and 2 dc), I dc into each of last 3 [3: 5: 5: 7] dc, turn.

Row 5: I ch (does NOT count as st), I dc into each of first 2 [2: 4: 4: 6] dc, miss I dc, (5 dc into next 4-ch sp, 7 dc into next 6-ch sp) 3 times, 5 dc into next 4-ch sp, miss I dc, I dc into next 3 dc, miss I dc, (5 dc into next 4-ch sp, 7 dc into next 6-ch sp) 3 times, 5 dc into next 4-ch sp, miss I dc, I dc into each of last 2 [2: 4: 4: 6] dc, turn.

Row 6: I ch (does NOT count as st), I dc into each of first I [I: 3: 3: 5] dc, I ch, miss 3 dc, I dc into next dc, 2 ch, miss 2 dc, I tr into next dc, (I picot, miss I dc, I tr into next dc) 3 times, 2 ch, miss 2 dc, I dc into next dc, 2 ch, miss 2 dc, I tr into next dc, (I picot, miss I dc, I tr into next dc) 3 times, 2 ch, miss 2 dc, I dc into next dc, 2 ch, miss 2 dc, I tr into next dc, (I picot, miss I dc, I tr into next dc) 3 times, 2 ch, miss 2 dc, I dc into next dc, I ch, miss 7 dc, I dc into next dc, 2 ch, miss 2 dc, I tr into next dc, (I picot, miss I dc, I tr into next dc) 3 times, 2 ch, miss 2 dc, I dc into next dc, 2 ch, miss 2 dc, I tr into next dc, (I picot, miss I dc, I tr into next dc) 3 times, 2 ch, miss 2 dc, I dc into next dc, 2 ch, miss 2 dc, I tr into next dc, (I picot, miss I dc, I tr into next dc) 3 times, 2 ch, miss 2 dc, I dc into next dc, I ch, miss 3 dc, I dc into each of last I [I: 3: 3: 5] dc, turn.

Row 7: 6 ch (counts as I qtr), miss st at base of 6 ch, (I qtr into next dc) 0 [0: 2: 2: 4] times, I dtr into first picot, 3 ch, I tr into next picot, 2 ch, I htr into next picot, 3 ch, I dc into next picot, 2 ch, I ss into next picot, 2 ch, I dc into next picot, 3 ch, I htr into next picot, 2 ch, I tr into next picot, 2 ch, I dtr into next picot, miss I ch sp, I qtr into next ch sp (the ch sp lying above 7 dc of row 5), I dtr into next picot, 3 ch, I tr into next picot, 2 ch, I htr into next picot, 3 ch, I dc into next picot, 2 ch, I ss into next picot, 2 ch, I dc into next picot, 3 ch, I htr into next picot, 2 ch, I tr

into next picot, 2 ch, I dtr into next picot, miss 2 ch sps, I qtr into each of last I [I: 3: 3: 5] dc, turn.

Row 8: I ch (does NOT count as st), I dc into each st to end.
Fasten off.

MAKING UP
Press as described on the information page.
Join both shoulder seams using back stitch, or mattress stitch if preferred.

Neckband
With RS facing, using 2¾mm (US 2) needles and yarn A, starting and ending at top of last row of crochet trim, pick up and knit 15 sts across top (row-end edge) of right front crochet trim, 21 [21: 23: 23: 25] sts up right side of front neck, and 7 sts down right side of back neck, K across 34 [34: 36: 36: 38] sts on back holder inc I st at centre, pick up and knit 7 sts up left side of back neck, 21 [21: 23: 23: 25] sts down left side of front neck, and 15 sts from top (row-end edge) of left front crochet trim. 121 [121: 127: 127: 133] sts.
Row I (WS): KI, *PI, KI, rep from * to end.
Row 2: As row I.
These 2 rows form moss st.
Work in moss st for a further 3 rows, ending with RS facing for next row.
Cast off in moss st.

Hem trim
With RS facing, using 2¾mm (US 2) needles and yarn A, starting and ending at centre dc of corner group of 3 dc across lower edge of last row of crochet trim, pick up and knit 233 [257: 281: 305: 333] sts evenly across entire hem edge of body.
Work in moss st as given for neckband for 5 rows, ending with RS facing for next row.
Cast off in moss st.

Button band
With RS facing, using 2¾mm (US 2) needles and yarn A, pick up and knit 135 [135: 135: 161: 161] sts evenly down left front opening edge, between cast-off edges of neckband and hem trim.
Work in moss st as given for neckband for 5 rows, ending with RS facing for next row.
Cast off in moss st.

Buttonhole band
Work to match button band, picking up sts up right front opening edge and with the addition of 7 buttonholes in row 2 as folls:
Row 2 (RS): Moss st 16 [16: 16: 18: 18] sts, *work 2 tog, yrn (to make a buttonhole), moss st 17 [17: 17: 21: 21] sts; rep from * 5 times more, work 2 tog, yrn (to make 7th buttonhole), moss st 3 sts.

Cuff trims (both alike)
With RS facing, using 2¾mm (US 2) needles and yarn A, pick up and knit 51 [51: 55: 55: 59] sts evenly across top of last row of sleeve crochet trim.
Work in moss st as given for neckband for 5 rows, ending with RS facing for next row.
Cast off in moss st.
Join sleeve seams. Insert sleeves into armholes. Sew on buttons.
See information page for finishing instructions.

joining point between motifs, yoh and draw loop through, (yoh and draw through 2 loops) 6 times, rep from * to * once more working into next picot, yoh and draw through all 4 loops on hook; **picot** = 3 ch, 1 ss into 3rd ch from hook; **qtr** = quadruple treble; **sp(s)** = space(s); **ss** = slip stitch; **tr** = treble; **tr2tog** = (yoh and insert hook as indicated, yoh and draw loop through, yoh and draw through 2 loops) twice, yoh and draw through all 3 loops on hook; **tr3tog** = (yoh and insert hook as indicated, yoh and draw loop through, yoh and draw through 2 loops) 3 times, yoh and draw through all 4 loops on hook; **tr4tog** = (yoh and insert hook as indicated, yoh and draw loop through, yoh and draw through 2 loops) 4 times, yoh and draw through all 5 loops on hook; **yoh** = yarn over hook.

BACK
Centre section
Using 4½mm (US 7) needles cast on 105 sts.
Beg with a K row, work in st st for 19 cm, ending with RS facing for next row.
Cast off.

FINNOULA

● ● ●

One size only
Rowan Felted Tweed Aran
            12 x 50gm
(photographed in Clay 777)

Knitting needles and crochet hook
1 pair 4mm (no 8) (US 6) needles
1 pair 4½mm (no 7) (US 7) needles
4.50mm (no 7) (US 7) crochet hook

Tension
18½ sts and 24 rows to 10 cm measured over st st using 4½mm (US 7) needles. Each large motif meas 19 cm square using 4.50mm (US 7) crochet hook.

Crochet abbreviations
ch = chain; **dc** = double crochet; **dtr2tog** = *(yoh) twice and insert hook as indicated, yoh and draw loop through, (yoh and draw through 2 loops) twice; rep from * once more, yoh and draw through all 3 loops on hook; **dtr3tog** = *(yoh) twice and insert hook as indicated, yoh and draw loop through, (yoh and draw through 2 loops) twice; rep from * twice more, yoh and draw through all 4 loops on hook; **joining st** = *(yoh) 4 times and insert hook into next picot, yoh and draw loop through, (yoh and draw through 2 loops) 4 times*, (yoh) 6 times and insert hook into

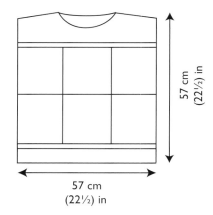

57 cm
(22½) in

57 cm
(22½) in

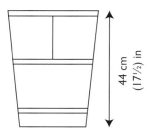

44 cm
(17½) in

Hem border

With RS facing and using 4.50mm (US 7) crochet hook, attach yarn to one end of cast-on edge of centre section, 1 ch (does NOT count as st), then work 97 dc evenly along entire cast-on edge (this is approx 1 dc for every cast-on st, missing 8 sts evenly across), turn. 97 sts.

Next row (WS): 4 ch (counts as 1 tr and 1 ch), miss first 2 dc, 1 tr into next dc, *1 ch, miss 1 dc, 1 tr into next dc; rep from * to end, turn.

Next row: 1 ch (does NOT count as st), 1 dc into each tr and ch sp to end, working last dc into 3rd of 4 ch at beg of previous row.
Fasten off.

Hem rib

With RS facing and using 4mm (US 6) needles, pick up and knit 105 sts evenly across top of last row of hem border (this is approx 1 st for every dc and 8 extra).

Row 1 (WS): P3, *K3, P3, rep from * to end.
Row 2: K3, *P3, K3, rep from * to end.
These 2 rows form rib.
Cont in rib until this section meas 6 cm from pick-up row, ending with RS facing for next row.
Cast off in rib.

Yoke border

Work exactly as given for hem border but working along cast-off edge of centre section.

Yoke

With RS facing and using 4½mm (US 7) needles, pick up and knit 105 sts evenly across top of last row of yoke border (this is approx 1 st for every dc and 8 extra).
Beg with a P row, work in st st until **entire** back section meas 54 cm **from cast-off edge of hem rib**, ending with RS facing for next row.

Shape shoulders

Cast off 6 sts at beg of next 6 rows. 69 sts.

Shape back neck

Next row (RS): Cast off 7 sts, K until there are 10 sts on right needle and turn, leaving rem sts on a holder.
Work each side of neck separately.
Cast off 3 sts at beg of next row.
Cast off rem 7 sts.
With RS facing, rejoin yarn and cast off centre 35 sts, K to end.
Complete to match first side, reversing shapings.

BASIC MOTIF 1

Using 4.50mm (US 7) crochet hook, make 5 ch and join with a ss to form a ring.

Round 1 (RS): 3 ch (does NOT count as st), tr3tog into ring, (5 ch, tr4tog into ring) 3 times, 5 ch, ss to top of tr3tog at beg of round.

Round 2: Ss into first ch sp, 3 ch (counts as 1 tr), 11 tr into same ch sp, (miss tr4 tog, 12 tr into next ch sp) 3 times, ss to top of 3 ch at beg of round. 48 sts.

Round 3: 1 ch (does NOT count as st), 1 dc between last tr of round 2 and 3 ch at beg of that round, *7 ch, tr2tog into 4th ch from hook, miss 3 tr of round 2, tr3tog between tr just missed and next tr, 4 ch, tr2tog into 4th ch from hook**, 3 ch, miss 3 tr of round 2, 1 dc between tr just

missed and next tr; rep from * to end, ending last rep at **, miss 3 tr of round 2, 1 tr into dc at beg of round.

Round 4: *5 ch, 1 ss into ch at base of next tr2tog, 3 ch, (1 ss, 3 ch, tr3tog, 3 ch and 1 ss) into top of next tr3tog, 3 ch, 1 ss into top of next tr2tog; rep from * to end. (Around this round there should be 8 "flowers", with each "flower" made up of 4 "petals", and between each "flower" there is a 5-ch sp.)

Round 5: Ss across and into centre of first 5-ch sp, 1 ch (does NOT count as st), 1 dc into this first 5-ch sp, *5 ch, 1 dc into top of next tr3tog of round 4, 5 ch, 1 dc into next 5-ch sp; rep from * to end, replacing dc at end of last rep with ss to first dc. 16 ch sps.

Round 6: 1 ch (does NOT count as st), miss st at base of 1 ch, *7 dc into next 5-ch sp, 1 picot; rep from * to end, ss to first dc.
Fasten off.
Completed basic motif 1 is an octagon shape – at each point there is a picot and there is another picot midway along each of the 8 sides.

BASIC MOTIF 2

Using 4.50mm (US 7) crochet hook, make 6 ch and join with a ss to form a ring.

Round 1 (RS): 3 ch (counts as 1 tr), 15 tr into ring, ss to top of 3 ch at beg of round. 16 sts.

Round 2: 1 ch (does NOT count as st), 1 dc into st at base of 1 ch, *2 ch, miss 1 tr, 1 dc into next tr; rep from * to end, replacing dc at end of last rep with ss to first dc. 8 ch sps.

Round 3: Ss into first 2-ch sp, 4 ch (does NOT count as st), dtr2tog into same first 2-ch sp, *5 ch, miss 1 dc**, dtr3tog into next 2-ch sp; rep from * to end, ending last rep at **, ss to top of dtr2tog at beg of round.

Round 4: Ss into first 5-ch sp, 4 ch (does NOT count as st), (dtr2tog, 5 ch and dtr3tog) into same first 5-ch sp, *5 ch, miss 1 dtr3tog**, (dtr3tog, 5 ch and dtr3tog) into next 5-ch sp; rep from * to end, ending last rep at **, ss to top of dtr2tog at beg of round.

Round 5: Ss into first 5-ch sp, 4 ch (does NOT count as st), (dtr2tog, 2 ch, dtr3tog, 2 ch and dtr3tog) into same first 5-ch sp, *7 ch, miss one 5-ch sp**, (dtr3tog, 2 ch, dtr3tog, 2 ch and dtr3tog) into next 5-ch sp; rep from * to end, ending last rep at **, ss to top of dtr2tog at beg of round.

Round 6: 1 ch (does NOT count as st), 1 dc into st at base of 1 ch, *2 dc into next 2-ch sp, 1 dc into next dtr3tog, 1 picot, 2 dc into next 2-ch sp, 1 dc into next dtr3tog, (3 dc, 1 picot and 3 dc) into next 7-ch sp**, 1 dc into next dtr3tog; rep from * to end, ending last rep at **, ss to first dc.
Fasten off.
Completed basic motif 2 is an octagon shape – at each point there is a picot and there is another picot midway along each of the 8 sides.
When joining motifs 1 and 2, join motifs whilst working last round by replacing the "3 ch" of each picot with "1 ch, 1 ss into corresponding picot of adjacent motif, 1 ch".

BASIC MOTIF 3

These motifs fill in the spaces between basic motifs 1 and 2 – see diagram. Make and join basic motifs 1 and 2 as detailed before making these motifs, as they are attached to the picots and joining points of the joined motifs whilst working last round.

Using 4.50mm (US 7) crochet hook, make 6 ch and join with a ss to form a ring.

Round 1 (RS): 3 ch (does NOT count as st), tr2tog into ring, (2 ch, tr3tog into ring) 7 times, 2 ch, ss to top of tr2tog at beg of round.

Now following diagram, join this motif to basic motifs 1 and 2 as shown in diagram as folls:

Round 2: 5 ch, miss st at base of 5 ch, 1 ss into motif joining point 1 on diagram, 5 ch, 1 ss into next tr3tog of round 1, 3 ch, 1 ss into picot of joined motifs at point 2 on diagram, 3 ch, 1 ss into next tr3tog of round 1, 5 ch, 1 ss into motif joining point 3 on diagram, 5 ch, 1 ss into next tr3tog of round 1, 3 ch, 1 ss into picot of joined motifs at point 4 on diagram, 3 ch, 1 ss into next tr3tog of round 1, 5 ch, 1 ss into motif joining point 5 on diagram, 5 ch, 1 ss into next tr3tog of round 1, 3 ch, 1 ss into picot of joined motifs at point 6 on diagram, 3 ch, 1 ss into next tr3tog of round 1, 5 ch, 1 ss into motif joining point 7 on diagram, 5 ch, 1 ss into next tr3tog of round 1, 3 ch, 1 ss into picot of joined motifs at point 8 on diagram, 3 ch, 1 ss into same place as ss at end of round 1.
Fasten off.

FRONT

Centre section

Make and join 6 motifs as shown in diagram – make 3 each of basic motif 1 and basic motif 2. Join these motifs whilst working last rounds as detailed above. Once these 6 motifs are made and joined, fill in the spaces as on diagram by working basic motif 3 – make 2 of these motifs, joining them to the other motifs as detailed above.

Using 4.50mm (US 7) crochet hook, attach yarn to point A on diagram and, working into picots and joining points of motifs, work straightening row across upper edge of joined motif panel as folls:

Next row (RS): 7 ch (does NOT count as st), 1 qtr into next picot, *7 ch, (1 dc into next picot, 5 ch) twice, 1 dc into next picot, 7 ch**, 1 **joining st** (see special abbreviations) into next picot, joining point and foll picot of adjacent motif; rep from * once more, then from * to ** again, 1 qtr into next picot, 7 ch, 1 ss into next picot.
Fasten off.

In same way, work across lower edge of motif panel.

Using 4.50mm (US 7) crochet hook, attach yarn to point B on diagram and, working into picots and joining points of motifs, work straightening row across side edge of joined motif panel as folls: *(5 ch, 1 dc into next picot) twice**, 7ch, 1 **joining st** (see special abbreviations) into next picot, joining point and foll picot of adjacent motif, 7 ch, 1 dc into next picot, rep from * to ** once more.
Fasten off.

In the same way, work across the opposite side of motif panel.

Hem border

With RS facing and using 4.50mm (US 7) crochet hook, attach yarn to a qtr at one end of straightening row along lower edge of centre section and work as folls: 1 ch (does NOT count as st), 1 dc into qtr at base of 1 ch, 9 dc into first 7-ch sp, (7 dc into each of next two 5-ch sps, 9 dc into each of next two 7-ch sps) twice, 7 dc into each of next two 5-ch sps, 9

dc into last 7-ch sp, turn. 97 sts.
Complete as given for hem border of back from **.

Hem rib

Work as given for hem rib of back.

Yoke border

Work exactly as given for hem border but working along upper edge of centre section.

Yoke

Work as given for yoke of back to beg of shoulder shaping, ending with RS facing for next row.

Shape shoulders

Cast off 6 sts at beg of next 2 rows. 93 sts.

Shape front neck

Next row (RS): Cast off 6 sts, K until there are 24 sts on right needle and turn, leaving rem sts on a holder.
Work each side of neck separately.
Dec 1 st at neck edge of next 4 rows **and at same time** cast off 6 sts at beg of 2nd row, then 7 sts at beg of foll alt row.
Work 1 row.
Cast off rem 7 sts.
With RS facing, rejoin yarn and cast off centre 33 sts, K to end.
Complete to match first side, reversing shapings.

SLEEVES (worked from top downwards)

Motif section

Make and join 2 basic motifs – one each of basic motif 1 and 2. Join motifs in same way as for motif panel of front, and reverse position of motifs for second sleeve.

With RS facing and using 4.50mm (US 7) crochet hook, attach yarn to corresponding point A of diagram on these motifs and, working into picots and joining points of motifs, work straightening row across upper edge of joined motif panel as folls:

Next row (RS): 7 ch (does NOT count as st), 1 qtr into next picot, *7 ch, (1 dc into next picot, 5 ch) twice, 1 dc into next picot, 7 ch**, 1 joining st (see special abbreviations) into next picot, joining point and foll picot of adjacent motif, rep from * to ** once more, 1 qtr into next picot, 7 ch, 1 ss into next picot.
Fasten off.

In same way, work across lower edge of joined motifs.

Top border

With RS facing and using 4.50mm (US 7) crochet hook, attach yarn to a qtr at one end of straightening row along upper edge of motif section and work as folls: 1 ch (does NOT count as st), 1 dc into qtr at base of 1 ch, 9 dc into first 7-ch sp, 7 dc into each of two 5-ch sps, 9 dc into each of next two 7-ch sps, 7 dc into each of next two 5-ch sps, 9 dc into last 7-ch sp, turn. 65 sts.
Complete as given for hem border of back from **.

Lower border

Work exactly as given for top border but working along lower edge of motif section.

Knitted section

With RS facing and using 4½mm (US 7) needles, pick up and knit 71 sts evenly across top of last row of lower border (this is approx 1 st for every dc and 6 extra).

Beg with a P row, work in st st as folls:

Work 1 row, ending with RS facing for next row.

Dec 1 st at each end of next and every foll alt row until 37 sts rem.

Work 1 row, ending with RS facing for next row.

Cast off.

Cuff border

With RS facing and using 4.50mm (US 7) crochet hook, attach yarn to one end of cast-off edge of knitted section, 1 ch (does NOT count as st), then work 37 dc evenly along entire cast-off edge (this is 1 dc for every cast-off st), turn. 37 sts.

Complete as given for hem border of back from **.

Cuff rib

With RS facing and using 4mm (US 6) needles, pick up and knit 36 sts evenly across top of last row of cuff border (this is 1 st for every dc minus 1 st).

Row 1 (WS): *K3, P3, rep from * to end.

This row forms the rib.

Cont in rib until this section meas 2.5 cm from pick-up row, ending with RS facing for next row.

Cast off **loosely** in rib.

MAKING UP

Press as described on the information page.

Join right shoulder seam.

Neckband

With RS facing and using 4.50mm (US 7) crochet hook, attach yarn to neck edge at left front shoulder and work edging row around entire neck edge as folls:

Edging row (RS): 1 ch (does NOT count as st), work 45 dc evenly around entire front neck edge, then 38 sts evenly around entire back neck edge, turn. 83 sts.

Complete as given for hem border of back from **.

With RS facing and using 4mm (US 6) needles, pick up and knit 87 sts evenly across top of last row of neck border (this is approx 1 st for every dc plus 4 extra).

Beg with row 1, work in rib as given for hem rib of back until this section meas 2 cm from pick-up row, ending with RS facing for next row.

Cast off **loosely** in rib.

Join left shoulder and neckband seams. Mark points along side seam edges 20 cm either side of shoulder seams, then sew upper edge of sleeves to body between these points. Join side and sleeve seams.

See information page for finishing instructions.

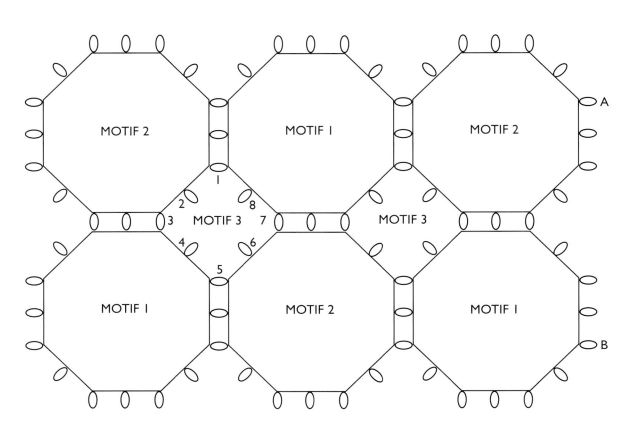

through all 3 loops on hook; **dtr3tog** = *(yoh) twice and insert hook as indicated, yoh and draw loop through, (yoh and draw through 2 loops) twice; rep from * twice more, yoh and draw through all 4 loops on hook; **htr** = half treble; **motif joining st** = yoh and insert hook into next dc, yoh and draw loop through, yoh and draw through 2 loops, (yoh) twice, insert hook into ss joining motifs and draw loop through, (yoh and draw through 2 loops) twice, miss corner dc of next motif, yoh and insert hook into next dc along edge of this motif, yoh and draw loop through, yoh and draw through 2 loops, yoh and draw through all 4 loops on hook; **neck joining st** = (yoh) 4 times and insert hook into next dc, yoh and draw loop through, (yoh and draw through 2 loops) 4 times, (yoh) 5 times, miss 1 dc and insert hook into next dc, yoh and draw loop through, (yoh and draw through 2 loops) 5 times, (yoh) 6 times, miss 2 dc and insert hook into next dc, yoh and draw loop through, (yoh and draw through 2 loops) 6 times, (yoh) 6 times, miss marked corner dc of this motif and marked corner dc of motif across base of neck, insert hook into next dc, yoh and draw loop through, (yoh and draw through 2 loops) 6 times, (yoh) 5 times, miss 2 dc and insert hook into next dc, yoh and draw loop through, (yoh and draw through 2 loops) 5 times, (yoh) 4 times, miss 1 dc and insert hook into next dc, yoh and draw loop through, (yoh and draw through 2 loops) 4 times, yoh and draw through all 7 loops on hook; **picot** = 3 ch, 1 ss into 3rd ch from hook; **sp(s)** = space(s); **ss** = slip stitch; **tr** = treble; **tr2tog** = (yoh and insert hook as indicated, yoh and draw loop through, yoh and draw through 2 loops) twice, yoh and draw

MEARA

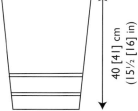

	S-M	L-XXL	
To fit bust	81-97	102-127	cm
	32-38	40-50	in
Rowan Felted Tweed			
A Treacle 145	8	10	× 50gm
B Cinnamon 175	1	1	× 50gm
C Barn Red 196	2	2	× 50gm
D Ancient 172	2	2	× 50gm
E Camel 157	1	1	× 50gm

Needles and crochet hook
1 pair 2¾mm (no 12) (US 2) needles
1 pair 3mm (no 11) (US 2/3) needles
2.50mm (no 12) (US B1/C2) crochet hook

Tension
25 sts and 36 rows to 10 cm measured over st st using 3mm (US 2/3) needles. Crochet motif is 10 cm square using 2.50mm (US B1/C2) crochet hook.

Crochet abbreviations
ch = chain; **dc** = double crochet; **dtr** = double treble; **dtr2tog** = *(yoh) twice and insert hook as indicated, yoh and draw loop through, (yoh and draw through 2 loops) twice; rep from * once more, yoh and draw

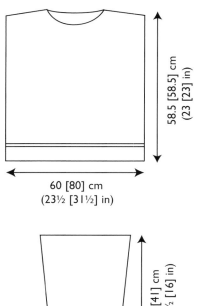

58.5 [58.5] cm
(23 [23] in)

60 [80] cm
(23½ [31½] in)

40 [41] cm
(15½ [16] in)

through all 3 loops on hook; **tr3tog** = (yoh and insert hook as indicated, yoh and draw loop through, yoh and draw through 2 loops) 3 times, yoh and draw through all 4 loops on hook; **ttr** = triple treble; **yoh** = yarn over hook.

BASIC CROCHET MOTIF

Using 2.50mm (US B1/C2) crochet hook and yarn E, make 6 ch and join with a ss to form a ring.

Round 1 (RS): 1 ch (does NOT count as st), 12 dc into ring, ss to first dc. 12 sts.

Breaking off and joining in colours as required, cont as folls:

Round 2: Using yarn B, 5 ch (counts as 1 tr and 2 ch), miss st at base of 5 ch, *1 tr into next dc, 2 ch; rep from * to end, ss to 3rd of 5 ch at beg of round.

Round 3: Using yarn C, (1 ss, 4 ch and dtr2tog) into first 2-ch sp, *4 ch, dtr3tog into next 2-ch sp; rep from * to end, replacing dtr3tog at end of last rep with ss to top of dtr2tog at beg of round.

Round 4: Using yarn D, 1 ch (does NOT count as st), 1 dc into st at base of 1 ch, *1 picot, 5 dc into next 4-ch sp**, 1 dc into next dtr3tog; rep from * to end, ending last rep at **, ss to first dc. Fasten off.

Round 5: Using yarn A, attach yarn to centre dc of one group of 5 dc, 1 ch (does NOT count as st), 1 dc into st where yarn was rejoined, *7 ch, miss (3 dc, 1 picot and 2 dc), 1 dc into next dc; rep from * to end, replacing dc at end of last rep with ss to first dc.

Round 6: Using yarn A, 1 ch (does NOT count as st), miss st at base of 1 ch, *9 dc into next 7-ch sp, 6 dc into next 7-ch sp, 7 ch (for corner loop), 1 dc into next 7-ch sp, turn, working back around round work 3 dc into same 7-ch sp as used for last dc, 3 dc into next 7-ch sp – this 7-ch sp already has 6 dc worked into it, turn, work 9 dc into corner 7-ch loop, then work 6 dc into 7-ch sp after this loop – this 7-ch sp already has 3 dc worked into it; rep from * to end, ss to first dc.

Motif is now a square, with 9 dc worked into each corner ch sp. Along centre of each side there are also 9 dc worked into a ch sp, and there are 6 dc worked into each ch sp between corner and centre ch sps.

Round 7: Using yarn A, 1 ch (does not count as st), *1 dc into each of next 9 dc, 1 dc into each of next 6 dc, 1 dc into each of next 9 corner dc (place marker on 5th of these 9 dc to mark corner point), 1 dc into each of next 6 dc; rep from * to end, ss to first dc. Fasten off.

In each corner of motif there is now a marked dc and there are 29 dc between each marked corner dc – 120 dc all round motif.

When joining motifs to form a band of motifs, join motifs whilst working round 7 by replacing the first joining corner block "9 dc" with "6 dc, 1 ss into corresponding dc of corner block of previous motif, 3 dc" and the second (last) corner block of "9 dc" with "3 dc, 1 ss into corresponding dc of corner block of previous motif, 6 dc". Along centre of sides of motifs join them by replacing the centre "9 dc" block with "5 dc, 1 ss into centre dc of corresponding centre block of adjacent motif, 4 dc".

When joining motifs to form a panel of motifs, join motifs whilst working

round 7 by replacing each corner block of "9 dc" with "(3 dc, 1 ss into corresponding dc of corner block of adjacent motif) twice, 3 dc". Along centre of sides of motifs, join them by replacing the "9 dc" block with "5 dc, 1 ss into centre dc of corresponding centre block of adjacent motif, 4 dc".

BACK

Motif band

Make and join 6 [8] motifs to form a band of motifs 6 [8] motifs long.

Hem stripe

***With RS facing, using 2.50mm (US B1/C2) crochet hook and yarn C, attach yarn to marked corner dc at one end of motif band and work along one long edge of motif band as folls:

Row 1 (RS): 3 ch (does NOT count as st), miss marked dc at base of 3 ch, 1 tr into next dc, 3 ch, miss 2 dc, *(tr3tog over next 3 dc, 3 ch, miss 2 dc) 5 times**, 1 motif joining st (see special abbreviations), 3 ch, miss 2 dc of next motif after st used for last "leg" of joining st; rep from * to end, ending last rep at **, tr2tog over next 2 dc (second of these 2 dc is marked corner dc at other end of motif band, turn. 36 [48] 3-ch sps.

Row 2: 1 ch (does NOT count as st), 1 dc into tr at base of 1 ch, *3 dc into next 3-ch sp, 1 dc into next st; rep from * to end, omitting 3 ch at beg of previous row, turn. 145 [193] sts.***

Break off yarn C and join in yarn D.

Row 3: 4 ch (counts as 1 tr and 1 ch), miss dc at base of 4 ch and next dc, 1 tr into next dc, *1 ch, miss 1 dc, 1 tr into next dc; rep from * to end, turn.

Row 4: 1 ch (does NOT count as st), 1 dc into st at base of 1 ch, *1 dc into next ch sp, 1 dc into next tr; rep from * to end, working dc at end of last rep into 3rd of 4 ch at beg of previous row, turn.

Break off yarn D and join in yarn E.

Row 5: 1 ch (does NOT count as st), 1 dc into each dc to end. Fasten off.

Hem rib

With RS facing, using 2¾mm (US 2) needles and yarn A, pick up and knit 150 [198] sts evenly along top of last crochet row. (This is approx 1 st for every dc of row 5, working twice into 5 dc evenly across.)

Row 1 (WS): P2, *K2, P2, rep from * to end.

Row 2: K2, *P2, K2, rep from * to end.

These 2 rows form rib.

Cont in rib until hem rib meas 6 cm from pick-up row, ending with RS facing for next row.

Cast off in rib.

Main section

Work along upper edge of motif band as given for hem stripe from *** to ***.

Break off yarn C and join in yarn A.

Row 3: 1 ch (does NOT count as st), 1 dc into each dc to end. Fasten off.

With RS facing, using 3mm (US 2/3) needles and yarn A, pick up and knit 150 [198] sts evenly along top of last crochet row. (This is approx 1 st for every dc, working twice into 5 dc evenly across.)

Beg with a P row, work in st st until back meas 57.5 cm from cast-off edge of hem rib, ending with RS facing for next row.

Shape back neck

Next row (RS): K53 [77] and turn, leaving rem sts on a holder.

Work each side of neck separately.

Dec 1 st at neck edge of next 3 rows, ending with RS facing for next row.

Cast off rem 50 [74] sts.

With RS facing, slip centre 44 sts onto a holder (for neckband), rejoin yarn and K to end.

Complete to match first side, reversing shapings.

FRONT

Motif panel

Make and join 28 [38] motifs to form shape shown in diagram.

(**Note:** Shaded motifs are only required for size L-XXL.)

Hem stripe

Work as given for hem stripe of back, working across lower edge of motif panel.

Hem rib

Work as given for hem rib of back.

Neck trim

With RS facing, using 2.50mm (US B1/C2) crochet hook and yarn A, attach yarn to marked corner st of motif at point A on diagram and work around front neck edge as folls:

Filling row (RS): 1 ch (does NOT count as st), 1 dc into marked dc at base of 1 ch, *1 dc into each of next 5 dc, miss 1 dc, 1 dc into each of next 6 dc, miss 1 dc, 1 htr into next dc, 1 tr into next dc, 1 dtr into next dc, dtr2tog over next 2 dc, 1 dtr into next dc, miss 1 dc, 1 ttr into next dc, ttr2tog over next 2 dc, 1 neck joining st (see special abbreviations) over rem 7 dc along side of this motif and first 7 dc along edge of next motif, ttr2tog over next 2 dc, 1 ttr into next dc, miss 1 dc, 1 dtr into next dc, dtr2tog over next 2 dc, 1 dtr into next dc, 1 tr into next dc, 1 htr into next dc, (miss 1 dc, 1 dc into each of next 6 dc) twice – last dc of this second group of 6 dc is worked into marked corner dc of motif*, 1 dc into marked corner dc of next motif, rep from * to * once more. 78 sts.

Fasten off.

SLEEVES

Motif band

Make and join 2 motifs to form a band motifs long.

With RS facing, using 2.50mm (US B1/C2) crochet hook and yarn A, attach yarn to marked corner dc at one end of motif band and work along one short edge of motif band as folls:

First side shaping row (RS): 1 ch (does NOT count as st), 1 dc into dc at base of 1 ch, 1 dc into next dc, miss 1 dc, 1 dc into each of next 4 dc, miss 1 dc, 1 htr into each of next 4 dc, (miss 1 dc, 1 tr into each of next 4 dc) twice, miss 1 dc, 1 dtr into each of next 4 dc, miss 1 dc, 1 dtr into each of next 3 dc – last of these sts is worked into marked corner dc (this is now top of motif band), turn.

Size L-XXL only

Next row: 3 ch (counts as 1 tr), miss st at base of 3 ch, 1 tr into each st to end.

Both sizes

Fasten off.

With RS facing, using 2.50mm (US B1/C2) crochet hook and yarn A, attach yarn to marked corner dc at top of other end of motif band and work along other short edge of motif band as folls:

Second side shaping row (RS): 4 ch (counts as 1 dtr), miss st at base of 4 ch, 1 dtr into each of next 2 dc, miss 1 dc, 1 dtr into each of next 4 dc, (miss 1 dc, 1 tr into each of next 4 dc) twice, miss 1 dc, 1 htr into each of next 4 dc, miss 1 dc, 1 dc into each of next 4 dc, miss 1 dc, 1 dc into each of next 2 dc – last of these sts is worked into marked corner dc, turn.

Size L-XXL only

Next row: 3 ch (counts as 1 tr), miss st at base of 3 ch, 1 tr into each st to end.

Both sizes

Fasten off.

Cuff stripe

With RS facing, using 2.50mm (US B1/C2) crochet hook and yarn C, attach yarn to corner of lower (shorter) edge of motif band and work along this edge of motif band and side shaping rows as folls:

Row 1 (RS): 3 ch (counts as 1 tr), miss point where yarn was rejoined, 0 [2] tr into row-end edge of side shaping row(s), tr2tog over marked corner dc of motif and next dc, 3 ch, miss 2 dc, *(tr3tog over next 3 dc, 3 ch, miss 2 dc) 5 times**, 1 motif joining st (see special abbreviations), 3 ch, miss 2 dc of next motif after st used for last "leg" of joining st, rep from * to ** once more, dtr2tog over next dc and marked corner dc at other end of motif band, 1 [3] tr into row-end edge of side shaping row(s), turn.

Row 2: 1 ch (does NOT count as st), 1 dc into tr at base of 1 ch, 1 dc into each of next 1 [3] sts, (3 dc into next 3-ch sp, 1 dc into next st) 12 times, 1 dc into each of last 1 [3] sts, working last dc into top of 3 ch at beg of previous row, turn. 51 [55] sts.

Break off yarn C and join in yarn D.

Row 3: 4 ch (counts as 1 tr and 1 ch), miss dc at base of 4 ch and next dc, 1 tr into next dc, *1 ch, miss 1 dc, 1 tr into next dc; rep from * to end, turn.

Row 4: 1 ch (does NOT count as st), 1 dc into st at base of 1 ch, *1 dc into next ch sp, 1 dc into next tr; rep from * to end, working dc at end of last rep into 3rd of 4 ch at beg of previous row, turn.

Break off yarn D and join in yarn E.

Row 5: 1 ch (does NOT count as st), 1 dc into each dc to end.

Fasten off.

Cuff rib

With RS facing, using 2¾mm (US 2) needles and yarn A, pick up and knit 54 [58] sts evenly along top of last crochet row. (This is approx 1 st for every dc of row 5, working twice into 3 dc evenly across.)

Beg with row 1, work in rib as given for hem rib until cuff rib meas 2 cm from pick-up row, ending with RS facing for next row.

Cast off in rib.

Main section

With RS facing, using 2.50mm (US B1/C2) crochet hook and yarn C, attach yarn to corner of upper (longer) edge of motif band and work along this edge of motif band and side shaping rows as folls:

Row 1 (RS): 3 ch (counts as 1 tr), miss point where yarn was rejoined, 2 [4] tr into row-end edge of side shaping row(s), dtr2tog over marked corner dc of motif and next dc, 3 ch, miss 2 dc, *(tr3tog over next 3 dc,

3 ch, miss 2 dc) 5 times**, 1 motif joining st (see special abbreviations), 3 ch, miss 2 dc of next motif after st used for last "leg" of joining st, rep from * to ** once more, dtr2tog over next dc and marked corner dc at other end of motif band, 3 [5] tr into row-end edge of side shaping row(s), turn.

Row 2: 1 ch (does NOT count as st), 1 dc into tr at base of 1 ch, 1 dc into each of next 3 [5] sts, (3 dc into next 3-ch sp, 1 dc into next st) 12 times, 1 dc into each of last 3 [5] sts, working last dc into top of 3 ch at beg of previous row, turn. 55 [59] sts.

Break off yarn C and join in yarn A.

Row 3: 1 ch (does NOT count as st), 1 dc into each dc to end.

Fasten off.

With RS facing, using 3mm (US 2/3) needles and yarn A, pick up and knit 59 [63] sts evenly along top of last crochet row. (This is approx 1 st for every dc, working twice into 4 dc evenly across.)

Beg with a P row, now work in st st as folls:

Inc 1 st at each end of 2nd and foll 7 [15] alt rows, then on 13 [10] foll 4th rows. 101 [115] sts.

Cont straight until sleeve meas 40 [41] cm from cast-off edge of cuff rib, ending with RS facing for next row.

Cast off.

MAKING UP

Press as described on the information page.

Join right shoulder seam using back stitch, or mattress stitch if preferred.

Neckband

With RS facing, using 2¾mm (US 2) needles and yarn A, pick up and knit 70 sts evenly along top of front neck filling row (this is 1 st for every dc missing 8 sts evenly), then 4 sts down right side of back neck, K across 44 sts on back holder, then pick up and knit 4 sts up left side of back neck. 122 sts.

Beg with row 1, work in rib as given for hem rib of back for 2 cm, ending with RS facing for next row.

Cast off in rib.

Join left shoulder and neckband seam. Mark points along side seam edges 20 [23] cm either side of shoulder seams, then sew cast-off edge of sleeves to back and front between these points. Join side and sleeve seams.

See information page for finishing instructions.

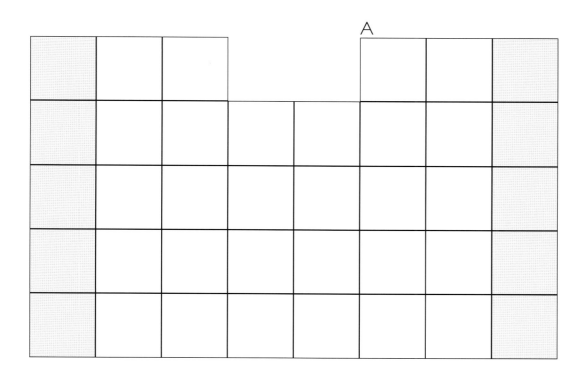

A

WHITE SQUARES ONLY = S-M
WHITE & GREY SQUARES = L-XXL

NIAMH

	S-M	L-XL	XXL	
To fit bust	81-97	102-117	122-127	cm
	32-38	40-46	48-50	in
Rowan Felted Tweed				
A Seafarer 170	2	3	3	x 50gm
B Treacle 145	2	2	2	x 50gm
C Bilberry 151	2	2	2	x 50gm
D Tawny 186	2	2	3	x 50gm
E Barn Red 196	2	3	3	x 50gm

Needles and crochet hook

1 pair 2¾mm (no 12) (US 2) needles
3.00mm (no 11) (US C2/D3) crochet hook

Tension

5 patt reps (25 sts) to **11** cm and 5 patt reps (10 rows) to **9** cm measured over patt using 3.00mm (US C2/D3) crochet hook.

Crochet abbreviations

ch = chain; **dtr** = double treble; **sp(s)** = space(s); **tr** = treble.

BACK and FRONT (both alike)
Using 2¾mm (US 2) needles and yarn A cast on 150 [178: 194] sts.
Row 1 (RS): K2, *P2, K2, rep from * to end.

Row 2: P2, *K2, P2, rep from * to end.
These 2 rows form rib.
Work in rib for a further 20 rows, ending with RS facing for next row.
Row 23 (RS): Rib 2 [8: 8], work 2 tog, (rib 10 [14: 14], work 2 tog) 12 [10: 11] times, rib 2 [8: 8]. 137 [167: 182] sts.
Cast off in rib (on **WS**) but do NOT fasten off.
Slip last loop from needles onto 3.00mm (US C2/D3) crochet hook and, working into sts of cast-off edge, cont as folls:
Foundation row (RS): 3 ch (counts as first st), miss st at base of 3 ch (this is last st of previous row), 1 tr into next st, *3 ch, miss 3 sts, 1 tr into each of next 2 sts; rep from * to end, turn. 27 [33: 36] patt reps.
Now work in patt as folls:
Row 1 (WS): 3 ch (counts as 1 tr), miss st at base of 3 ch and next tr, *5 tr into next ch sp**, miss 2 tr; rep from * to end, ending last rep at **, miss 1 tr, 1 tr into top of 3 ch at beg of previous row, turn.
Row 2: 3 ch (counts as 1 tr), miss st at base of 3 ch, 1 tr into next tr, *3 ch, miss 3 tr, 1 tr into each of next 2 tr; rep from * to end, working tr at end of last rep into top of 3 ch at beg of previous row, turn.
These 2 rows form patt.
Cont in patt for a further 3 rows, ending with RS facing for next row.
Break off yarn A and join in yarn B.
Work in patt for 10 [12: 12] rows.
Break off yarn B and join in yarn C.
Work in patt for 10 [12: 12] rows.

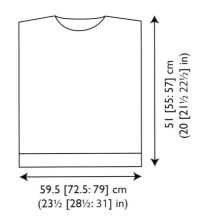

51 [55: 57] cm
(20 [21½: 22½] in)

59.5 [72.5: 79] cm
(23½ [28½: 31] in)

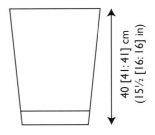

40 [41: 41] cm
(15½ [16: 16] in)

Break off yarn C and join in yarn D.
Work in patt for 10 [12: 12] rows.
Break off yarn D and join in yarn E.
Completing work using yarn E only, cont as folls:
Work 12 [10: 12] rows, ending with RS facing for next row. (Work should meas approx 49 [53: 55] cm.)

Shape neck
Next row (RS): 3 ch (counts as 1 tr), miss st at base of 3 ch, 1 tr into next tr, (3 ch, miss 3 tr, 1 tr into each of next 2 tr) 8 [11: 12] times, 2 ch, miss 3 tr, 1 dtr into next tr and turn, leaving rem sts unworked.
Next row: 3 ch (counts as 1 tr), miss dtr at base of 3 ch, 2 tr into first ch sp, *miss 2 tr, 5 tr into next ch sp, rep from * to last 2 sts, miss 1 tr, 1 tr into top of 3 ch at beg of previous row. 8½ [11½: 12½] patt reps.
Fasten off.
Return to last complete row worked, miss centre 45 [45: 50] tr, rejoin yarn to next tr and cont as folls:
Next row (RS): 6 ch (counts as 1 dtr and 2 ch), miss st where yarn was rejoined and next 3 tr, *1 tr into each of next 2 tr**, 3 ch, miss 3 tr; rep from * to end, ending last rep at ** and working last tr of this last rep into top of 3 ch at beg of previous row, turn.
Next row: 3 ch (counts as 1 tr), miss st at base of 3 ch and next tr, (5 tr into next ch sp, miss 2 tr) 8 [11: 12] times, 2 tr into last ch sp, 1 tr into 4th of 6 ch at beg of previous row. 8½ [11½: 12½] patt reps.
Fasten off.

SLEEVE STRIPE SEQUENCE
After knitted rib has been completed, work crochet section in stripes as folls:
Foundation row and foll 5 rows: Using yarn A.
Next 8 rows: Using yarn B.
Next 8 rows: Using yarn C.
Next 8 rows: Using yarn D.
Rem rows: Using yarn E.

SLEEVES
Using 2¾mm (US 2) needles and yarn A cast on 50 [54: 58] sts.
Work in rib as given for back and front for 23 rows, dec 3 [2: 1] sts evenly across last row and ending with **WS** facing for next row. 47 [52: 57] sts.
Cast off in rib (on **WS**) but do NOT fasten off.
Slip last loop from needles onto 3.00mm (US C2/D3) crochet hook and, working into sts of cast-off edge, cont as folls:
Working in sleeve stripe sequence throughout (see above), work foundation row as given for back and front. 9 [10: 11] patt reps.
Now work in patt as given for back and front as folls:
***Work 2 rows.
Row 3 (WS): 3 ch (counts as 1 tr), 1 tr into st at base of 3 ch – 1 st increased, miss 1 tr, *5 tr into next ch sp**, miss 2 tr; rep from * to end, ending last rep at **, miss 1 tr, 2 tr into top of 3 ch at beg of previous row – 1 st increased, turn.
Row 4: 3 ch (counts as 1 tr), miss st at base of 3 ch, 1 tr into each of next 2 tr, *3 ch, miss 3 tr, 1 tr into each of next 2 tr; rep from * to last st, 1 tr into top of 3 ch at beg of previous row, turn.

Row 5: 3 ch (counts as 1 tr), 1 tr into st at base of 3 ch – 1 st increased, 1 tr into next tr, miss 1 tr, *5 tr into next ch sp**, miss 2 tr; rep from * to end, ending last rep at **, miss 1 tr, 1 tr into next tr, 2 tr into top of 3 ch at beg of previous row – 1 st increased, turn.
Row 6: 4 ch (counts as 1 tr and 1 ch), miss st at base of 4 ch and next tr, 1 tr into each of next 2 tr, *3 ch, miss 3 tr, 1 tr into each of next 2 tr; rep from * to last 2 sts, 1 ch, miss 1 tr, 1 tr into top of 3 ch at beg of previous row, turn.
Row 7: 3 ch (counts as 1 tr), 1 tr into st at base of 3 ch – 1 st increased, 2 tr into next ch sp, miss 2 tr, *5 tr into next ch sp, miss 2 tr; rep from * to last 2 sts, 2 tr into next ch sp, 2 tr into 3rd of 4 ch at beg of previous row – 1 st increased, turn.
Row 8: 5 ch (counts as 1 tr and 2 ch), miss st at base of 5 ch and next 2 tr, 1 tr into each of next 2 tr, *3 ch, miss 3 tr, 1 tr into each of next 2 tr; rep from * to last 3 sts, 2 ch, miss 2 tr, 1 tr into top of 3 ch at beg of previous row, turn.
Row 9: 3 ch (counts as 1 tr), 1 tr into st at base of 3 ch – 1 st increased, 3 tr into next ch sp, miss 2 tr, *5 tr into next ch sp, miss 2 tr; rep from * to last 3 sts, 3 tr into next ch sp, 2 tr into 3rd of 5 ch at beg of previous row – 1 st increased, turn.
Row 10: 6 ch (counts as 1 tr and 3 ch), miss st at base of 6 ch and next 3 tr, 1 tr into each of next 2 tr, *3 ch, miss 3 tr, 1 tr into each of next 2 tr; rep from * to last 4 sts, 3 ch, miss 3 tr, 1 tr into top of 3 ch at beg of previous row, turn.
Row 11: 3 ch (counts as 1 tr), miss st at base of 3 ch, 5 tr into next ch sp – 1 st increased, miss 2 tr, *5 tr into next ch sp, miss 2 tr; rep from * to last 4 sts, 5 tr into next ch sp, 1 tr into 3rd of 6 ch at beg of previous row – 1 st increased, turn.
Row 12: 3 ch (counts as 1 tr), miss st at base of 3 ch, 1 tr into next tr, *3 ch, miss 3 tr, 1 tr into each of next 2 tr; rep from * to end, working tr at end of last rep into top of 3 ch at beg of previous row, turn.
11 [12: 13] patt reps.
Rep from *** twice more. 15 [16: 17] patt reps.
Cont straight until sleeve meas approx 40 [41: 41] cm, ending with RS facing for next row.
Fasten off.

MAKING UP
Press as described on the information page.
Join right shoulder seam.
Neckband
With RS facing, using 2¾mm (US 2) needles and yarn E, pick up and knit 5 sts down left side of front neck, 49 [49: 51] sts from front, 5 sts up right side of front neck, 5 sts down right side of back neck, 49 [49: 51] sts from back, and 5 sts up left side of back neck. 118 [118: 122] sts.
Beg with row 2, work in rib as given for back and front for 7 rows, ending with RS facing for next row.
Cast off in rib.
Join left shoulder and neckband seam. Mark points along side seam edges 17 [19: 20] cm either side of shoulder seams, then sew sleeves to body between these points. Join side and sleeve seams.
See information page for finishing instructions.

STRIPE SEQUENCE
Row 1: Using yarn A.
Row 2: Using yarn B.
Row 3: Using yarn C.
Row 4: Using yarn D.
Row 5: Using yarn E.
Row 6: Using yarn F.
These 6 rows form stripe sequence and are repeated throughout.

BACK

Using 3.50mm (US E4) crochet hook and yarn A make
103 [113: 127: 139: 155] ch.

Foundation row: 1 dc into 2nd ch from hook, 1 dc into each ch to end,
turn. 102 [112: 126: 138: 154] sts.

Beg with stripe sequence row 2 (see above), now work in patt as folls:

Row 1 (RS): 1 ch (does NOT count as st), 1 dc into each dc to end, turn.
This row forms patt.

Cont in patt in stripe sequence until back meas 34 [35: 36: 37: 38] cm.

Shape armholes

Keeping stripes correct, cont as folls:

Next row: Ss across and into 6th [7th: 8th: 9th: 10th] st, 1 ch (does NOT
count as st), 1 dc into st at base of 1 ch – 5 [6: 7: 8: 9] sts decreased, 1 dc
into each dc to last 5 [6: 7: 8: 9] dc and turn, leaving rem 5 [6: 7: 8: 9] dc

SIOBHAN

	S	M	L	XL	XXL	
To fit bust	81-86	91-97	102-107	112-117	122-127	cm
	32-34	36-38	40-42	44-46	48-50	in

Rowan Felted Tweed

A Ancient 172	2	3	3	3	3	× 50gm
B Granite 191	2	2	3	3	3	× 50gm
C Stone 190	2	2	2	3	3	× 50gm
D Delft 194	2	2	2	3	3	× 50gm
E Cinnamon 175	2	2	2	3	3	× 50gm
F Barn Red 196	2	2	2	3	3	× 50gm

Crochet hook

3.50mm (no 9) (US E4) crochet hook

Fastenings – 1 decorative pin-brooch

Tension

22 sts and 24 rows to 10 cm measured over patt using 3.50mm (US E4)
crochet hook.

Crochet abbreviations

ch = chain; **dc** = double crochet; **dc2tog** = (insert hook as indicated, yoh
and draw loop through) twice, yoh and draw through all 3 loops; **yoh** =
yarn over hook.

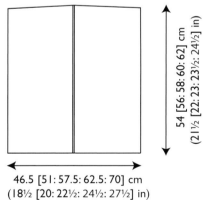

46.5 [51: 57.5: 62.5: 70] cm
(18½ [20: 22½: 24½: 27½] in)

54 [56: 58: 60: 62] cm
(21½ [22: 23: 23½: 24½] in)

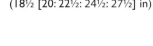

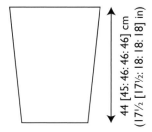

44 [45: 46: 46: 46] cm
(17½ [17½: 18: 18: 18] in)

unworked - 5 [6: 7: 8: 9] sts decreased. 92 [100: 112: 122: 136] sts.
Next row: 1 ch (does NOT count as st), dc2tog over first 2 sts – 1 st decreased, 1 dc into each dc to last 2 sts, dc2tog over last 2 sts – 1 st decreased, turn.
Working all decreases as set by last row, dec 1 st at each end of next 4 [4: 6: 7: 8] rows, then on foll 4 [5: 6: 7: 9] alt rows.
74 [80: 86: 92: 100] sts.
Cont straight until armhole meas 18 [19: 20: 21: 22] cm.
Shape shoulders
Keeping stripes correct, cont as folls:
Next row: Ss across and into 4th [5th: 5th: 6th: 6th] st, 1 ch (does NOT count as st), 1 dc into st at base of 1 ch – 3 [4: 4: 5: 5] sts decreased, 1 dc into each dc to last 3 [4: 4: 5: 5] dc and turn, leaving rem 3 [4: 4: 5: 5] dc unworked - 3 [4: 4: 5: 5] sts decreased.
Rep last row 1 [3: 1: 3: 0] times more. 62 [48: 70: 52: 90] sts.
Next row: Ss across and into 5th [6th: 6th: 7th: 7th] st, 1 ch (does NOT count as st), 1 dc into st at base of 1 ch – 4 [5: 5: 6: 6] sts decreased, 1 dc into each dc to last 4 [5: 5: 6: 6] dc and turn, leaving rem 4 [5: 5: 6: 6] dc unworked - 4 [5: 5: 6: 6] sts decreased.
Rep last row 2 [0: 2: 0: 3] times more. 38 [38: 40: 40: 42] sts.
Fasten off.

RIGHT FRONT (worked sideways, beg at front opening edge)
Using 3.50mm (US E4) crochet hook and yarn A make 120 [124: 129: 133: 137] ch.
Work foundation row as given for back. 119 [123: 128: 132: 136] sts.
Beg with stripe sequence row 2 (see above), now work in patt as given for back and cont as folls:
Work 21 [21: 25: 25: 25] rows.
Working all shaping in same way as shaping is worked for back, cont as folls:
Dec 1 st at end of next row and at same edge on 4 foll 4th [5th: 4th: 5th: 6th] rows. 114 [118: 123: 127: 131] sts.
Work 1 [1: 3: 3: 3] rows, ending at hem edge.
Shape armhole
Dec 26 [26: 25: 24: 22] sts at end of next row.
88 [92: 98: 103: 109] sts.

Dec 2 sts at shaped end of next 2 [3: 5: 5: 6] rows, then 1 st at same edge of foll 9 [9: 9: 12: 14] rows. 75 [77: 79: 81: 83] sts.
Work 4 [5: 7: 8: 9] rows.
Fasten off.

LEFT FRONT (worked sideways, beg at front opening edge)
Work to match left front, reversing all shapings.

SLEEVES
Using 3.50mm (US E4) crochet hook and yarn A make 43 [45: 47: 47: 49] ch.
Work foundation row as given for back. 42 [44: 46: 46: 48] sts.
Beg with stripe sequence row 2 (see above), now work in patt as given for back and cont as folls:
Work 4 [4: 4: 3: 3] rows.
Next row: 1 ch (does NOT count as st), 2 dc into first dc – 1 st increased, 1 dc into each dc to last dc, 2 dc into last dc – 1 st increased, turn. 44 [46: 48: 48: 50] sts.
Working all increases as set by last row, inc 1 st at each end of 5th [5th: 5th: 4th: 4th] and every foll 6th [5th: 5th: 5th: 4th] row to 74 [56: 66: 86: 62] sts, then on every foll – [6th: 6th: -: 5th] row until there are - [78: 82: -: 90] sts.
Cont straight until sleeve meas 44 [45: 46: 46: 46] cm.
Shape top
Working all shaping in same way as for back armhole shaping, cont as folls:
Dec 5 [6: 7: 8: 9] sts at each end of next row. 64 [66: 68: 70: 72] sts.
Dec 1 st at each end of next 6 rows, then on every foll alt row until 40 sts rem, then on foll 10 rows. 20 sts.
Fasten off.

MAKING UP
Press as described on the information page.
Join both shoulder seams, positioning front opening edges so that they meet at centre back neck. Join side seams. Join sleeve seams. Insert sleeves into armholes.
See information page for finishing instructions.
Fasten fronts as in photograph using decorative pin-brooch.

KEELA JACKET

● ●

	S-M	L-XL	XXL	
To fit bust	81-97	102-117	122-127	cm
	32-38	40-46	48-50	in
Rowan Felted Tweed Aran & Felted Tweed				
A FTA Carbon 759	14	17	19	× 50gm
B *FT Delft 194	4	4	5	× 50gm
C FTA Granite 719	8	8	10	× 50gm
D FTA Scree 765	2	3	3	× 50gm

*USE FELTED TWEED DOUBLE THROUGHOUT

Crochet hook
4.50mm (no 7) (US 7) crochet hook

Tension
15 sts and 6½ rows to 10 cm measured over patt using 4.50mm (US 7) crochet hook.

Crochet abbreviations
ch = chain; **cluster** = (yoh, insert hook as indicated, yoh and raw loop through) 4 times – 9 loops on hook, yoh and draw through 8 loops, yoh and draw through rem 2 loops; **dc** = double crochet; **sp(s)** = space(s); **tr** = treble; **yoh** = yarn over hook.

STRIPE SEQUENCE
Rows 1 to 3: Using yarn A.
Row 4: Using yarn B.
Row 5: Using yarn A.
Row 6: Using yarn B.
Rows 7 to 9: Using yarn A.
Rows 10 and 11: Using yarn C.
Row 12: Using yarn D.
Rows 13 and 14: Using yarn C.
These 14 rows form stripe sequence and are repeated throughout.

BACK
Using 4.50mm (US 7) crochet hook and yarn A make 98 [114: 126] ch.
Foundation row (RS): 1 cluster into 4th ch from hook, *1 ch, miss 1 ch, 1 cluster into next ch; rep from * to last 2 ch, 1 ch, miss 1 ch, 1 tr into last ch, turn. 96 [112: 124] sts.
Beg with stripe sequence row 1 (see above – note that as stripe sequence starts with 3 rows using yarn A there will be 4 rows in total using yarn A at hem edge), now work in patt as folls:
Row 1: 3 ch (counts as 1 tr), miss tr at base of 3 ch, *1 cluster into next

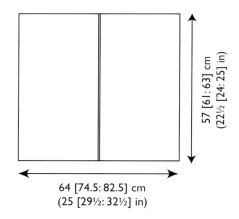

57 [61: 63] cm
(22½ [24: 25] in)

64 [74.5: 82.5] cm
(25 [29½: 32½] in)

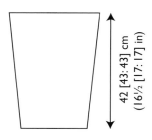

42 [43: 43] cm
(16½ [17: 17] in)

ch sp, 1 ch, miss 1 cluster; rep from * to last st, 1 tr into top of 3 ch at beg of previous row, turn.
This row forms patt.
Cont in patt until back meas 57 [61: 63] cm.
Fasten off.

LEFT FRONT
Using 4.50mm (US 7) crochet hook and yarn A make 50 [58: 64] ch.
Work foundation row as given for back. 48 [56: 62] sts.
Now work in patt in stripe sequence until left front matches back to fasten-off point.
Fasten off.

RIGHT FRONT
Work as given for left front.

SLEEVES
Using 4.50mm (US 7) crochet hook and yarn A make 38 [40: 42] ch.
Work foundation row as given for back. 36 [38: 40] sts.
Beg with stripe sequence row 1 (see above – note that as stripe sequence starts with 3 rows using yarn A there will be 4 rows in total using yarn A at hem edge), now work in patt as given for back as folls:
Work 1 row.
***Next row: 4 ch (counts as 1 tr and 1 ch), miss tr at base of 3 ch, *1 cluster into next ch sp**, 1 ch, miss 1 cluster; rep from * to end, ending last rep at **, 2 ch, miss 1 cluster, 1 tr into top of 3 ch at beg of previous row, turn.
Next row: 3 ch (counts as 1 tr), miss tr at base of 3 ch, (1 cluster, 1 ch and 1 cluster) into first 2-ch sp, 1 ch, miss 1 cluster, *1 cluster into next ch sp**, 1 ch, miss 1 cluster; rep from * to end, ending last rep at **, 1 ch, 1 tr into 3rd of 4 ch at beg of previous row, turn. 40 [42: 44] sts.
Work 3 [2: 2] rows.

Rep from *** 3 [4: 4] times more, and then first 2 of these rows (the inc rows) again. 56 [62: 64] sts.
Cont straight until sleeve meas 42 [43: 43] cm.
Fasten off.

MAKING UP
Press as described on the information page.
Join both shoulder seams, positioning front opening edges so that they meet at centre back neck.
Front band
With RS facing, using 4.50mm (US 7) crochet hook and yarn A, attach yarn at base of right front opening edge.
Using the "3 ch" or "1 tr" of row-end edges as the "ch sps" and working approx 3 sts for each pair of row-end edges, work up entire right front opening edge as folls: 3 ch (counts as 1 tr), (1 cluster into edge, 1 ch) 42 [45: 47] times, 1 cluster into edge (this should be at top of right front opening edge at centre back neck), now work down entire left front opening edge as folls: (1 ch, 1 cluster into edge) 41 [44: 46] times, 1 ch, 1 tr into edge (this should be base of left front opening edge), turn.
170 [182: 190] sts.
Now work in patt as given for back as folls:
Work 2 rows.
Break off yarn A and join in yarn C.
Work 1 row.
Break off yarn C and join in yarn A.
Next row (RS): 1 ch (does NOT count as st), 1 dc into each cluster and ch sp to end.
Fasten off.
Mark points along side seam edges 20 [22: 23] cm either side of shoulder seams, then sew sleeves to body between these points. Join side and sleeve seams.
See information page for finishing instructions.

CLOSE UPS

These detailed images are a reference tool to aid
with making each design.

Caitlin

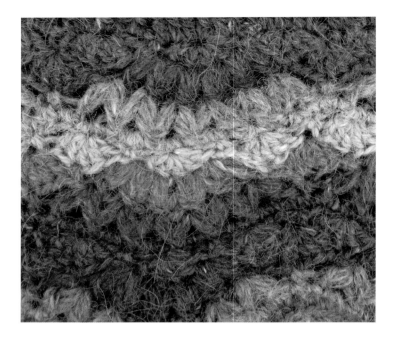

Caitlin

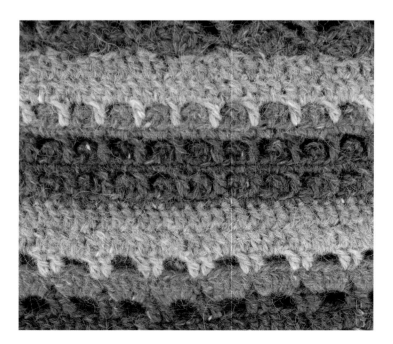

Catriona

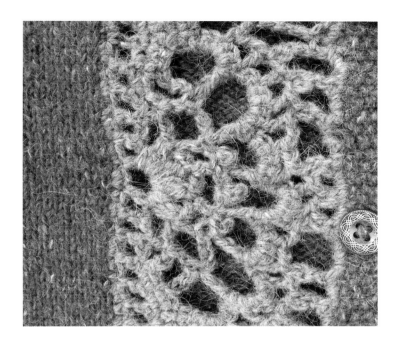

Finnoula

Catriona

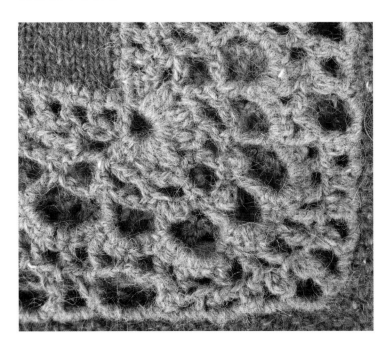

Finnoula

Gael

Meara

Gael

Meara

Keela Jacket

Niamh

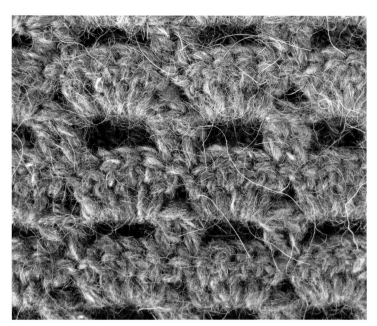

Siobhan

Niamh

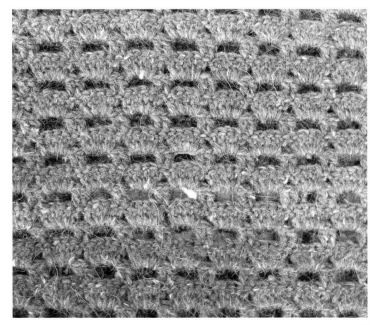

TENSION

Achieving the correct tension is one of the most important factors when knitting one of my designs. I cannot stress highly enough that you really do need to knit a tension square BEFORE you start to knit the garment. The tension stated on each of my patterns must be achieved to ensure that the garment fits correctly and that it matches the measurements stated on the size diagram. I recommend that you knit a square using the number of stitches and rows stated on the pattern tension plus 3 or 4 stitches and rows. To check your tension, place the knitted square on a flat surface and mark out a 10cm square using pins as markers. Count the number of stitches and rows between the pins. If you have too many stitches, then your knitting is too tight, knit another square using a thicker needle. If you have too few stitches, then your knitting is too loose, knit another square using a thinner needle. It is also important to keep checking your tension whilst you are knitting your garment especially if you are returning to knit after leaving your work for a period of time.

SIZING

The patterns are written giving the instructions for the smallest size, for the other sizes work the figures in the brackets. The measurements stated on the size diagrams are the measurements of your finished garment AFTER pressing.

MODEL SIZE

Georgia is 5'8'' tall and is a standard size 8/10 and she is wearing the smallest size in each photograph.

FINISHING

Finishing your garment beautifully is another important factor when making one of my designs. Good finishing will ensure that your garment fits correctly and washes and wears well. I urge you to spend time pressing and stitching your garment together, after all you've just spent a lot money and time knitting it using lovely Rowan yarns and the last thing you want to do is ruin it with bad finishing!

PRESSING

Firstly sew in any loose ends to the wrong side of the knitting. Block out each piece of knitting and then press according to the care instructions stated on the yarn ball bands. Always press using an iron on the wrong side of the knitting over a protective cloth (this can be damp or dry) and have the steam setting switched on the iron. Pay particular attention to the sides or edges of each piece as this will make the sewing up both easier and neater. Take special care with the welts and cuffs of the knitting – if the garment is fitted then gently steam the ribs so that they fill out but remain elastic. If the garment is a boxy, straight shape then steam press out the ribs to correct width.

STITCHING

When stitching the pieces together, remember to match areas of colour, texture or pattern very carefully where they meet. I recommend that you use mattress stitch wherever possible, this stitch gives the neatest finish ensuring that the seam lays flat.

Having knitted your pieces according to the pattern instructions, generally the shoulder seams of the front and back are now joined together using mattress stitch. Work the neck trim according to the pattern instructions and then join the neckband seams using mattress stitch if required. Knit neck bands or collars to the length stated in the pattern instructions, slightly stretching the trims before measuring if knitted in garter stitch or horizontal ribbing. Please take extra care when stitching the edgings and collars around the neck of the garment as these control the stretch of the neck. The sleeves are now normally added to the garment, take care to match the centre of the sleeve head to the shoulder seam. Ideally stretch the sleeve head into the armhole and stitch in place, if the sleeve head is too large for the armhole then check your tension as your knitting may be too loose. Join the underarm and side seams. Slip stitch any pockets or pocket lining into place and sew on buttons corresponding to the button holes lining up the outside edge of the button with the edging join or seam.

Carefully press your finished garment again to the measurements stated on the size diagram.

AFTERCARE

Ensure that you wash and dry your garment according to the care instructions stated on the yarn ball bands. If your garment uses more than one type of yarn then wash according to the most delicate. Reshape your garment when slightly damp and then carefully press to size again.

BUTTONS

The buttons used in this collection were kindly supplied by Bedecked Haberdashery:

Bedecked Haberdashery,
The Coach House,
Barningham,
Richmond,
North Yorkshire,
DL11 7DW
Tel: +44 (0) 1833 621451
Email: thegirls@bedecked.co.uk
Web: www.bedecked.co.uk

EXPERIENCE RATING

For guidance only.

● suitable for a beginner crocheter/knitter with a little experience.

● ● suitable for a crocheter/knitter with average ability.

● ● ● suitable for the experienced crocheter/knitter

CROCHET ABBREVIATIONS

The crochet patterns are written in the English style, however I am aware that the terminology varies from country to country. To help you, listed below are the English abbreviations with the US alternatives.

ENGLISH	US
ch chain	ch chain
dc double crochet	sc single crochet
htr half treble	hdc half double crochet
tr treble	dc double crochet
dtr double treble	tr treble

KNITTING ABBREVIATIONS

K	knit
P	purl
st(s)	stitch(es)
inc	increas(e)(ing)
dec	decreas(e)(ing)
st st	stocking stitch (1 row K, 1 row P)
g st	garter stitch (K every row)
beg	begin(ning)
foll	ollowing
rem	remain(ing)
rev st st	reverse stocking stitch (1 row K, 1 row P)
rep	repeat
alt	alternate
cont	continue
patt	pattern
tog	together
mm	millimetres
cm	centimetres
in(s)	inch(es)
RS	right side
WS	wrong side
sl 1	slip one stitch
psso	pass slip stitch over
p2sso	pass 2 slipped stitches over
tbl	through back of loop
M1	make one stitch by picking up the horizontal loop before the next stitch and knitting into the back of it
M1P	make one stitch by picking up the horizontal loop before the next stitch and purling into the back of it
yfwd	yarn forward
yrn	yarn round needle
meas	measures
0	no stitches, times or rows
-	no stitches, times or rows for that size
yon	yarn over needle
yfrn	yarn forward round needle
wyib	with yarn at back

Aiofe Scarf

Meave Wrap